John Ross Macduff

Saint Paul in Rome

Or the Teachings, Fellowships, and Dying Testimony of the Great Apostle in the City of the Caesars, Being Sermons Preached in Rome in the Spring of 1871

John Ross Macduff

Saint Paul in Rome
Or the Teachings, Fellowships, and Dying Testimony of the Great Apostle in the City of the Caesars, Being Sermons Preached in Rome in the Spring of 1871

ISBN/EAN: 9783744784924

Printed in Europe, USA, Canada, Australia, Japan

Cover: Foto ©Lupo / pixelio.de

More available books at **www.hansebooks.com**

SAINT PAUL
IN
ROME.

OR,

The Teachings, Fellowships, and Dying Testimony of the Great Apostle in the City of the Cæsars:

BEING

SERMONS PREACHED IN ROME IN THE SPRING OF 1871.

With an Introduction

BY

J. R. MACDUFF, D.D.

Author of "Memories of Gennesaret,"
"Memories of Bethany," &c.

Fourth Thousand.

"I am ready to preach the gospel to you that are at Rome also."—ROM. i. 15.
"And Paul dwelt two whole years in his own hired house, and received all that came in unto him, preaching the kingdom of God, and teaching those things which concern the Lord Jesus Christ, with all confidence, no man forbidding him."—ACTS xxviii. 30, 31.

LONDON
JAMES NISBET & CO., 21 BERNERS STREET
MDCCCLXXII

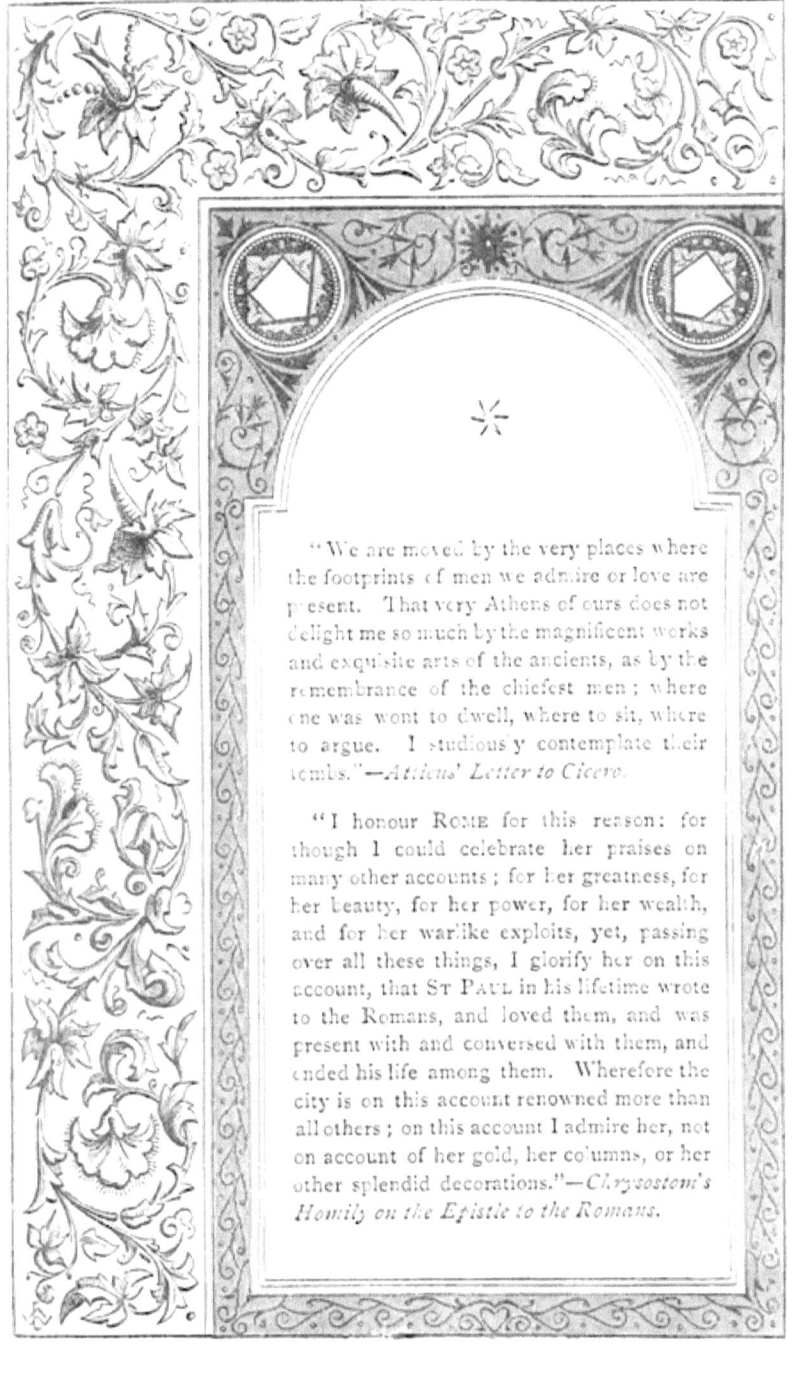

"We are moved by the very places where the footprints of men we admire or love are present. That very Athens of ours does not delight me so much by the magnificent works and exquisite arts of the ancients, as by the remembrance of the chiefest men; where one was wont to dwell, where to sit, where to argue. I studiously contemplate their tombs."—*Atticus' Letter to Cicero.*

"I honour ROME for this reason: for though I could celebrate her praises on many other accounts; for her greatness, for her beauty, for her power, for her wealth, and for her warlike exploits, yet, passing over all these things, I glorify her on this account, that ST PAUL in his lifetime wrote to the Romans, and loved them, and was present with and conversed with them, and ended his life among them. Wherefore the city is on this account renowned more than all others; on this account I admire her, not on account of her gold, her columns, or her other splendid decorations."—*Chrysostom's Homily on the Epistle to the Romans.*

To

J. Warrington Wood, Esq.,

Sculptor, Rome,

One of the Worshippers at the Porta del Popolo;

and who,

in the Great Art of which he is Master,

has consecrated his genius to the noblest ends;

𝕿𝖍𝖎𝖘 𝖁𝖔𝖑𝖚𝖒𝖊,

with true friendship and regard,

is

inscribed.

PREFACE.

THE Introduction which follows, is intended to stand for a Preface.

A word of apology may, however, be further premised, for the somewhat personal and colloquial style of that preliminary dissertation; also, for the apparent, indeed the acknowledged incongruity of its matter with what succeeds.

It may be sufficient to say, that there were not a few subjects of a topographical and traditional character bearing on my theme, and gleaned by personal observation and inquiry on the spot, which I considered might be of interest to the reader, as they unquestionably were to the writer. Moreover, that it were better to cast these alike in a familiar shape and separate opening chapter, rather than relegate them to footnotes, which are seldom read, or incorporate them with the pages of the Sermons,—thus leaving the latter to be given as they were delivered.

All the recent discoveries of Roman Archæology, as well as older ecclesiastical legends bearing on the Apostolic age, have a secondary, indeed, but not less real value for the Bible student and the Christian Church. Besides, they ought at least to deepen and augment the interest of any such themes and life-lessons as those which it has been attempted, most imperfectly, to illustrate in the second part of the volume, with reference to the closing years of the world's greatest benefactor.

The Discourses themselves were preached on eight successive Sabbaths, in fulfilment of a duty devolved upon the Author by the Church at home. Some of them will be found less directly, others more directly, bearing on St Paul's residence in the Imperial City.

September 1871.

*Picture of St Paul on an ancient glass cup in the Vatican Museum.
See Introductory Chapter, p. 12.*

CONTENTS.

	PAGE
INTRODUCTORY CHAPTER,	15

SERMON I.
ROM. i. 15, 16.
St Paul's Announcement of his Purpose in going to ROME, ... 102

SERMON II.
ROM. i. 15-17; PHIL. iii. 7-9.
St Paul's Letter to THE ROMANS: *Its Great Theme*, ... 126

SERMON III.
ROM. i. 7; 2 TIM. i. 2-5.
St Paul's Fellowships in ROME: TIMOTHY, . 154

SERMON IV.
2 TIM. iii. 15, 16; ACTS xxviii. 23.
The Bible in ROME.—*St Paul's Testimony to the Authority of Holy Scripture.—The Word of God not bound,* 188

SERMON V.

PHILEM. 9, 10.

St Paul's Converts in ROME : *among the Soldiers : among the poor and degraded.*—ONESIMUS ; *and the Epistle written from* ROME *to Philemon,* 220

SERMON VI.

PHIL. iv. 22.

St Paul's special Salutations from the Saints in CÆSAR'S *Household,* 250

SERMON VII.

2 TIM. i. 16-18 ; iv. 19.

St Paul's Prayer in ROME *for* ONESIPHORUS, 282

SERMON VIII.

2 TIM. i. 12 ; iv. 6-8.

St Paul's Dying Testimony in ROME.—*His Martyrdom.—Conclusion,* 314

INTRODUCTORY CHAPTER.

IN visiting for the first time the Eternal City, nothing, amid its thousand thronging recollections, was of such profound interest as the "Roman Memories of St Paul."

Circumstances interfered with the cherished purpose of making a preliminary acquaintance with the sites of "Appii Forum" and "The Three Taverns;" but we were able, under favourable auspices, including among these the brightest of skies, to trace the course of the Apostle-prisoner along the beautiful bay of Baiae, as the shores of Italy first opened upon him. If the commonly-accepted dates be correct, it must have been, too, about the same period of the year, when vine and fig-tree were in earliest bud; and the weeping willow, still so pleasingly familiar at this season to the traveller, was hanging its full, graceful tresses by the wayside. I felt it a privilege to stand on the only remaining step, covered with bright seaweed, and furrowed with age, on which he set foot at Puteoli,* also to follow him in thought in his journey to the capital, through the Arco Felice and by the Lake Avernus, till the ancient road, which in all probability he pursued, and which joins the Appian Way at Sinuessa, disappeared from our sight amid the rubbish and brushwood near Cumae.

The other termination of the great "Via Appia" (whose polygonal blocks of basalt are in many places still grooved with the wheels which, two thousand years ago, passed over them), formed one of our first resorts on reaching Rome itself. It is easily

The Via Appia at Rome.

---

* A church is close by, but erected not to St Paul but to the Virgin. St Januarius, whose name is associated with the pretended miracle of liquefied blood, is evidently the patron saint of modern 'Pozzuoli.'

accessible from the supposed site of the old Porta Capena of the Servian wall, by the modern San Sebastiano and Arch of Drusus.* However doubtful may be the identity of other traditional spots, which superstition has associated with St Paul, one fully realised his presence here. It was the feeling akin to what had previously been experienced, in a visit to Palestine, with regard to a Greater; when, amid the difficulties of tracing the Redeemer's footsteps in connection with other localities, we felt there could be no hesitation that we were on the most consecrated ground on earth, as we trod the green sward of Olivet, or the beach of Gennesaret.

We could, accordingly, vividly imagine the Apostle, accompanied with the band of Roman

---

* This original entrance to the Appian Way will more than likely be soon brought to light, if indeed the discovery is not already made. The well-known President of one of the Archæological Societies in Rome is now engaged in clearing the mounds of earth half way between the Baths of Caracalla and the Arch of Constantine, in search of the "missing link."

B

"Brethren" (some who met him at Appii Forum, and others, probably older and less able for the journey, who had joined them at "The Three Taverns"), now approaching the end of their long route of fifty-one miles. We may be pardoned for pausing, as we endeavour to picture and vivify the scene which then opened before the central figure of that group. Of all the entrances to ancient, as to modern Rome, this was incomparably the grandest. Well may the Appian have been boastfully named by Statius, *Regina Viarum* (the Queenly Way). It formed the great line of communication, not only with southern Italy, but with the most remote oriental possessions of the Cæsars, starting from the Golden Milestone in the Roman Forum and terminating at Brundusium. It was on nearing Rome it must have assumed its most imposing form and dimensions. Where now, for miles along this regal approach, we have only the fragments of grim, weather-stained sepulchres, wreathed with

St Paul's approach to the City.

acanthus and ivy, interspersed here and there with remains of mediæval fortresses, lonely blocks of travertine, and other masses of unshapely ruin,—there must have stretched before the Apostle's eye one long magnificent street, lined with monuments to illustrious dead; a vast colonnade of tombs, with no vault but the blue sky, forming, if we may venture on the comparison, the Westminster Abbey of the Imperial City,* while the present waste, treeless Campagna, which girdles the modern Rome as with a zone of death, was studded with patrician villas and palatial residences. The range of Alban and Sabine hills would appear on his

---

* All the burying-grounds in ancient times were extra-mural; situated generally in some conspicuous place immediately beyond the gates. I was struck with this peculiarity at Pompeii. The "Street of Tombs," outside one of the principal entrances, forms not the least interesting and noteworthy feature in the exhumed city. I noticed similar rows of ruined sepulchres, recently excavated, at Bayli and Cumae. The same, as every reader knows, was the case in Palestine. We have the familiar instance of the funeral of the Widow's Son, met as it was proceeding *outside* the gate of Nain. To this day, the Jerusalem Cemetery is the immemorial one in the Valley of Jehoshaphat.

right. Conspicuous above him would be Monte Cavi, whither the laurelled conquerors of Rome were wont to proceed in triumphal procession with their trophies from the Capitol,—the Temple of Jupiter Latialis, long supplanted by a modern Passionist Convent, crowning its summit. Not far off, he would see Frescati, on its gentle eminence, enshrined in olive groves; and still farther to the right, Tivoli, nestling in its purple shadows, with the mountains of the Abruzzi for a background. Farthest away of all would be snowy Soracte, the solitary guardian of the northern landscape. Other thoughts and themes may possibly have been burdening his spirit as he passed monuments which to this hour engross the interest of the Roman archæologist; a few, even then, hoary with age, others fresh from the chisel of sculptor or architect. Among the latter, on his right, would be that to the memory of the Consul Quintus Veranius. More conspicuous, alike in dimensions and splendour, would be the still surviving circular sepulchre, with its blocks of travertine—the Casale Rotondo, then recently erected by Augustus to the head of one of his great senatorial families. These two ancient tombs to the left, with their broad basement of peperino, are erected over the spot where, in the infancy of the empire, the Horatii and Curiatii fell. While here and there, mingling with this city of the dead, glimpses would be caught, through occasional openings, of the temples of Romulus, Bacchus, and Mars ; or, on a greater scale than all, of those enormous aqueducts, then in their completed vastness, whose weird colossal fragments, still spanning the naked "Prairie" of which we have spoken, form the most picturesque of all the relics of Rome's ancient splendour.

We may imagine the spot reached where the round tower of Cecilia Metella, built since St Paul's time, crowns a gentle descent. Here he would obtain his most impressive view of the city proper, as the Aventine and Palatine

Mounts more nearly revealed themselves, with their crowded piles of architecture,—whether Theatres or Basilicas, Baths or Arches, Temples or Palaces; and yet, discovering also streets of squalid misery, homes festering with poverty and crime, which, as much as in any city of the present day, were in strange juxtaposition with dwellings of luxurious and guilty extravagance. Nor can we fail, in passing, to note, that the modern traveller can discern from this point, what was all unknown to the illustrious wayfarer, the Campanile of the great Basilica (of which more hereafter), which is the traditional custodier of his own martyred ashes, and nigh the reputed spot where he sealed his testimony with his blood. He must have trodden too, at this same place, over ground, or immediately adjoining it, which was yet to have its own hallowed history and associations. To this history, and these associations indeed, in one sense, this memorable entry into the Imperial City gave birth; for a

The Basilica of San Paolo and the Catacombs.

few steps farther, on reaching the bottom of that gentle descent, he must have walked over one, if not more, of those vast subterranean vaults (dug probably originally to obtain stones and sand for the buildings of the city), whose tortuous caverns, in coming centuries, were to be utilised by the Christians as shelters for the persecuted living and graves for their martyred dead. As the great Apostle passed along that sepulchral road, could he fail to read on these monuments many inscriptions of aching hearts? —inscriptions similar to those which may still be seen preserved in the Lapidarian Museum of the Vatican, gathered from heathen Columbaria, —the mute agony of unsolaced grief, left to tell its tale of hopelessness and despair on the dumb stone or marble. All the boasted mythology of Rome was helpless to answer the question, "Shall the dust praise Thee?" That silent necropolis—the dormitory of the Infant Church —would yet utter through the rudest of epitaphs its cheering response—a response furnished and bequeathed by the Great Teacher who was now unconsciously passing over it—" Ye sorrow not as others who have *no hope.*"—" To die is gain."—" Them also that sleep in Jesus will God bring with Him!"

We can even, with no great effort of imagination, still further vivify the scene, by the introduction of lesser accessories; for the familiar surroundings of to-day are, many of them at least, identical with those which then greeted the eye of the Apostle. As he advanced on the crowded highway, he would see, in dress and customs, much of (what we may call) the ordinary routine of Roman life, which can have undergone little alteration since then. Yonder Contadini—peasants from the Alban hills, with their "pointed hats, their cloaks of undressed shaggy hides, rough sandals on their feet, and yellow gourds for water slung across their shoulders,"—would meet him, as they met us, going, as it might be, for Roman market or holiday: or that other group driving their

The Scene and its surroundings.

patient team—the horns of the oxen twined with wild flowers or scarlet fillets—would bestow a passing glance on the dust-covered traveller. There, Senator or Praetor in his toga, would be seen rattling along the pavement, with an attendant retinue of slaves, to his Sabine retreat: there, a wasted valetudinarian repairing for recruited strength to the sea breezes of Baiae or Cumae. There, is a turbaned Asiatic enjoying his first pilgrimage to the mistress of kingdoms. There, are the still indispensable fountains enshrined in semicircular seats, filled with loungers or wayfarers to and from the busy capital. Where that unsandalled Capuchin is walking dreamily along, counting his beads, or mumbling his missal, there might be a priest of Jupiter seen hastening to do sacrifice at Cavi or Egeria. Where these bronzed berseglieri, with quick movement, are hurrying on an embassy to Albano, he might encounter some Pretorian guards, or helmeted horsemen, returning to their barracks in the Palatine or Campus Martius. There, may have been another young Giotto tending his goats on the wayside, and watching the golden sunset behind these gaunt solemn cypresses, or cluster of stone pines. There, would be a swarm of irrepressible beggars, similar in look and gesture to those who still urge their importunate suits. Groups of children might be busied plucking the wild flowers, which then as now line the wayside, or culling the yellow-berried ivy from the walls. While the timid green lizard basking in the sunlight, would be seen hurrying away at the approaching footstep, and burying itself from sight in the nearest tiny aperture or cluster of drooping ferns.

Thus then St Paul is at the gates of ROME.
His arrival at the gates. And in saying so, the long dream of his life is at last fulfilled. It is the realisation of what forms, at one time, the incidental topic of his conversation with friends, "I must also see Rome" (Acts xix. 21), at others, the reiterated topic of a letter, " Having

a great desire these many years to come unto you" (Rom. xv. 23–33; also Rom. i. 10–15). A desire, moreover, which must have been mightily augmented and stimulated by such a sanction and promise as this, " Be of good cheer, Paul; for as thou hast testified of me in Jerusalem, so must thou bear witness also in ROME" (Acts xxiii. 11). Dare we fathom the thoughts which must have been burning within the bosom of the moral Hero, as he listened to the hum of all this busy industry and frivolous pleasure; and gazed, amid the triumphs of art and power, on visible evidences of Pagan ignorance and heathen depravity on every side? Would not his spirit, as on a kindred occasion, on entering the world's sister capital, be "stirred within him?" Would not his inmost resolve, though not expressed in words, be this,—" I can do all things through Christ strengthening me;" 'and among these all things, in God's great name, this impregnable citadel must be stormed and fall. Its ramparts, at whatever cost, must be carried, and its magazines redeemed for the service of "the Prince of the kings of the earth."' But enough. In silent emotion, the obscure, impotent, unknown Pilgrim from Asia Minor—the unnoted unit among the teeming throng—pursues his way, until, passing by the gate of the modern wall, onward by the narrow valley between the Cœlian and Aventine, along the *Via Triumphalis*, he gazes on the aggregate glories of the Palatine; and entering the Forum, the centre and focus of the great Babylon, with the Temple of Concord and Saturn in front, and that of Jupiter Tonans crowning the summit of the Capitoline, the ambassador in bonds is merged with his little company in that sea of multitudinous life!

We have no authentic records to guide us in following the cavalcade farther; nor is it my design, in this introductory chapter, to attempt entering into the details of St Paul's residence at Rome. This would not only far exceed our prescribed limits,

Design of Introductory Chapter.

but it would be, at best, only a feeble rehearsal of what has been so ably rendered by others. My purpose, rather, is to convey a few impressions, gathered recently on the spot, regarding localities associated with the great Apostle; and though some of these rest on no more than tradition, it may not be uninteresting to the reader, as it was to the writer, to know about them, and receive them for what they are worth. After the rejection of the spurious and legendary, there remains, at all events, an ample residuum of truth.

It would have been of the deepest interest to the Christian student had there been the possibility of ascertaining, with any degree of certainty, the situation of that memorable dwelling, or rather dwellings, of his; the "lodging" and "hired house." I made it my endeavour, while resident in the city, alike to explore the traditional sites of these, and to obtain regarding them the opinion of the most reliable antiquarian au-

St Paul's "lodging" and "hired house."

thorities whose acquaintance I was privileged to form.

I may here remark, once for all, as having reference to other Bible scenes and localities in Rome, that while there are to be found, regarding not a few of these, the wildest and most extravagant myths—delusions fortified with hosts of lying miracles, which can only provoke a smile, and are summarily to be repudiated—it would be unfair to involve all such in one indiscriminate rejection. The historical sites of Jerusalem (some of these more sacred still), are in many cases hopeless for identification; and for this obvious reason, that with every desire on the part of the Church of the early centuries to retain them in remembrance, siege after siege swept over the devoted city; and amid sack and pillage, and fire, and centuries of expulsion, all vestige of such 'holy places' was irretrievably obliterated. Amid similar ravages, on the other hand, which, in successive centuries wasted the

Value to be attached to traditionary sites.

Roman capital, there neither was any such material change in its natural features, nor any such extermination of those who alone had a sacred interest in transmitting to posterity an acquaintance with the spots dear to the hearts and memories of the faithful. The Christian Church, planted by the great Apostle in the city of the Cæsars, never ceased to exist; and a knowledge of those haunts—such as his hired lodging—his dungeon—the place of his martyrdom and death—all undoubtedly known to the early converts, could hardly fail to be confided, as a hallowed secret—a sacred legacy—from generation to generation. Nor, surely, have we any reason to impeach the accuracy and trustworthiness of the attesting witnesses. They would mark and cherish such localities, even when the power of the persecutor as yet forbade them, in any visible or tangible form, to perpetuate the memories which surrounded them; and when, on the establishment of Christianity throughout the empire, they could with impunity claim these as their own, can we doubt how jealously they would continue to guard them? Great seems the difference between their accurate conservation of sacred places, and the later extravagances of relics and miracles, which, as unnatural excrescences have grown out of and deformed them.

It was cherishing these feelings that I repaired, in the first instance, to the Church of "Santa Maria, Via Lata," in the Corso (adjoining the Doria Palace) —the reputed "House of St Paul." While the other prisoners who had accompanied him from Puteoli were taken, as was usual, to the Pretorian camp;—by a special act of considerate clemency (for which he was doubtless indebted to the influence and indulgence of Julius with the Prefect Burrhus), he was conducted, it is alleged, under guard to this temporary home. Here he would have that memorable interview with his countrymen so

"House of St Paul," Church of Santa Maria in Via Lata.

minutely described in the closing chapter of the Acts. Many thousands of these were resident in the Transtevere—the quarter in that age which corresponded with the modern Ghetto. The Church of Santa Maria was founded by Sergius in the eighth century, and rebuilt by Innocent VIII. in 1485.

A youth lit a small lamp and conducted us to a subterranean chamber, where he pointed to some unreliable frescoes alleged to be painted by St Luke. The position of the large stones under the archway adjoining the Via Lata, and which are of unmistakable antiquity, betoken that the street was at one time considerably below its present level. To the left hand, in entering the vault, is a pillar surmounted by a vase, said to contain martyrs' blood. The pillar was brought from the Catacombs of St Sebastian : an iron chain or fetter is suspended loose from the centre; above and below which, the appropriate words are inscribed in Latin, " SED VERBUM DEI NON EST

ALLIGATUM"* ("But the Word of God is not bound").

The main objection raised by some to the accuracy of this traditional spot is, that it occupies the site of the Septa Julia—an edifice built for the assemblies and votation of the Comitia, by Julius Cesar, B.C. 26. But there seems no great extravagance or unlikelihood in the assumption, that one of these smaller chambers, into which antiquarians tell us this "Government building" was divided, might have been appropriated for a few days to the reception of a political prisoner under custody of a state officer. This objection, moreover, would have been more feasible had the vault in the Via Lata been identified with St Paul's "own hired house," in which he resided "two whole years." For such a length of time, and with the unrestrained freedom we are expressly informed he enjoyed while there, in proclaiming

St Paul's "hired house," Church of S. Paolo allo Regola.

---

* See illustration on the binding of this Volume.

the truths of the Gospel, his residence could hardly fail to prove an inconvenience and interference in a public state building. But if we still farther follow out the ecclesiastical legend, the difficulty is removed. By a careful perusal of the narrative in the Acts, there is a strong probability that two separate dwelling-places are there referred to. In other words, that he was transferred from the place of his first and temporary domicile in the city, to some other permanent lodgment spoken of by the phrase, "his own hired house."*

Such a dwelling is pointed out within the Church which commemorates this place and period of his Roman life, "S. Paolo o Paolino allo Regola." Thither I went, at the suggestion of one specially conversant in questions relating to Christian Archæology. I discovered the

---

* There are two separate words employed, Ξενία and μισθωμα (Acts xxviii. 23, 30). Ξενία is only on one other occasion found in the New Testament and in Paul's writings—viz., when he says in his Epistle to Philemon, "prepare me also *a lodging*."

place with some difficulty; for the Church itself is comparatively little known, not having much of interest or impressiveness about its architecture, and being in rather an inaccessible situation, adjoining the Ghetto, not far from Ponte Sisto, and the ruins of the Theatre of Balbus.* Entering the Church, at the right of the Altar is a doorway, surmounted by the following inscription in black lettering:—"DIVI PAULI APOSTOLI HOSPITIUM ET SCHOLA." A few steps conduct down to an oblong apartment, said, from the above inscription, to be "The house and school of St Paul." Its windows at present look out to an extremely narrow street. Its walls are surrounded with marble slabs, on which are written, in Latin, appropriate verses from the Acts and Romans. For example, in descending, on the right hand, the eye is attracted with the words—

---

* It must frankly be owned, that subjects of classical and Pagan, rather than of Christian antiquity, are those which mainly engross the study of archæologists in Rome.

"SEQUENTE AUTEM NOCTE,
ASSISTENS EI DOMINUS
AIT,
CONSTANS ESTO,
SICUT ENIM TESTIFICATUS ES DE ME
IN JERUSALEM,
SIC TE OPORTET ET
ROMÆ.
ACTS XXIII. 11."

In the upper end of the chamber is a tolerably-executed picture of St Paul, with the simple inscription —

"PAULUS SERVUS JESU CHRISTI.

On either side are similar appropriate Latin inscriptions—one from Acts xxv. 12, the other from Acts xxv. 10, 11. In an old and curious volume shown me by an eminent resident archæologist, there is the following reference to this Church of Allo Regola, explaining how it came to be called the *School* of St Paul:— "Those he converted to Christ, here came to be catechised, because it was a retired site." *

---

* "*Tesori Nascosti dell' Alma Citta di Roma*," "Treasures

There always must necessarily be much uncertainty hanging over one or both of these "memorial buildings." But even allowing a wide margin for doubt, one could not help, in visiting their dim vaults, endeavouring to realise, at least the possibility, that the greatest of mere men—he whom Chrysostom, in one of his 'golden' epithets, truly calls "the Heart of the World"—once gazed on these walls; that here he gathered around him the nucleus of the Christian Church in the world's great capital; that here, according to the narrative in the Acts, he threw open his doors to all inquirers; rejected by the Jew, he turned with confident hope to the Gentile, and day after day, with unabating and unflagging

Interest connected with the Home of St Paul.

Concealed of the Beautiful City of Rome, MDCXXV." And yet, as an illustration of the gross delusions which are found side by side with more sober and reliable statements, it is added after the sentence just quoted, "In the year 1096, in a stone in this Church, was placed a list of relics of saints. Among these relics were the arm of St Paul; and the shoes of Christ, which the Great Baptist said he was unworthy to stoop down and unloose."

zeal, "from morning to evening," expounded to them "the unsearchable riches of Christ," — "teaching" as well as "preaching" (for both are specially conjoined, Acts xxviii. 31) the good news of the kingdom. Nay farther, according to the very strong and emphatic, we may even say, cheering and encouraging language which closes the record of the Acts, doing so without let or hindrance, "with all confidence, no man forbidding him;"* that here Aristarchus and Epaphras, his fellow-prisoners, may have gladdened him with their presence; that here Epaphroditus may have come to him with gifts from the Philippians; that here Luke may have written, under his supervision, the "Acts of the Apostles;" that here Onesiphorus may have come oft to refresh him; and Onesimus to be equipped for his City Mission work; and Timothy to receive

His oral instructions.

---

* Μετὰ πασης παρρησίας, ἀκολύτως, implying a remarkable exception, something not to have been expected.—*See Alford's Greek Testament.*

parental counsel, and yield in return, filial love; that here one of the soldiers, to whom by turns he was chained night and day, may have gone back to his barracks when his hour of duty expired, carrying the tale of this wondrous, self-sacrificing, noble-hearted criminal, from whose magnanimous soul love to God and man seemed ever to be gushing forth like a perennial stream, —recounting the words he there heard uttered, and the hymns he there heard sung,—words and hymns telling of ONE who seemed to combine the might and majesty of their own Olympian Jove with the tenderness of more than a human Friend;* that here, as in the case of his Great Master, "the common people" may have "heard him gladly." Numbers from the streets and lanes around, attracted by various motives, may have come to listen to the doctrines of the strange Jewish preacher, " and that which seemed at first," as it has

---

* See note on Graphite, in Collegio Romano, at the beginning of Sermon V.

been beautifully said, "to impede, must really have deepened the impression of his eloquence; for who could see, without emotion, that venerable form subjected by iron links to the control of the soldier who stood beside him? how often must the tears of the assembly have been called forth by the upraising of that fettered hand, and the clanking of the chain which checked its energetic action!"* Nor have we exhausted all the associations of that Roman dwell- *His written Epistles.* ing, when we remember, that in more ways than by his living voice, the world stands related to him as an everlasting debtor. There, he may possibly have dictated to his scribe, the greater number—we had almost said the most valuable—of his Epistles; those repertories of holy thought, which have proved as ministering angels to countless anxious, aching, sorrowing hearts. That dimly-lighted chamber may have been the little "Oracle" whence issued "responses" and behests for mankind—

---

* Howson and Conybeare's "St Paul," vol. ii. p. 387.

the "holy Church throughout all the world" his audience—all time the period of his influence,—thus making him the instructor of future centuries and unborn peoples. As the burning arrows went forth from his quiver, the modern pillar with its fetter and inscription seems faithfully to describe the joy of his free spirit, "An ambassador in bonds; *but the Word of God is not bound!*" What spot on earth, could we only know it with certainty, could be compared in interest with that? The eagles on those imperial standards with which then he may have become familiar, were winging their magnificent flight to the ends of the earth ; but that chained Eagle, by one of the bridges of the Tiber, was pluming his pinions for more majestic soarings. From that "hired house" was to go forth a power mightier than the behests of Cæsar, more irresistible than the shock of legions and cohorts. As it has been said, " The vast Roman empire, the most powerful on the face of the earth, which required seven ages to establish, this man takes only a quarter of an age to regenerate."*

We naturally pass from the reputed dwelling of the Apostle, to speak of those in the Roman capital with whom he was brought into contact; his friends, companions, and converts. *His companions and converts.* To make reference to all of these, even in the most cursory shape, would form far too wide a theme for a prefatory chapter. Some are selected for more special consideration in the sequel of this volume. It may be interesting, however, to note in passing, that among other remarkable discoveries in Christian Archæology, is that of slabs and sarcophagi—these too of the first century—found in the old places of sepulture, bearing a few of the very names of those to whom Paul sent his salutations in the 16th chapter of Romans.

---

* Monod. From the "hired house" must have been written the Epistles to Philemon, to the Colossians, to the Ephesians, and to the Philippians.

Many travellers can enter into the feelings so well expressed by Dr Howson, when he says, " He can never forget the start of pleasure with which he saw the name of Tryphæna in one of the cells underground, and then that of Tryphosa among the foliage in another part of the same vineyard. But many others of the identical names in the Epistle occur among these inscriptions. Some, indeed, such as Urban and Hermes, are common names, so as to cause no surprise; others, such as Stachys and Patrobas, are comparatively rare, so as to arrest the attention more; while such a combination as that of Philologus and Julia deserves special observation; the former word appearing among these monuments, and the latter in itself indicating a connection with the imperial family. On the whole, though nothing can be absolutely proved, it is difficult not to believe that we have here in modern Rome the ashes of some of those, in the midst of whose companionship St Paul preached the gospel in ancient Rome." I shall limit myself, at present, to a reference to two of these Roman friends and converts of St Paul, not only because their names are less known than others, but because, on account of comparatively recent excavations in the city, a new interest has gathered around them; I mean, the names, and I may add the households, of *Clement* and *Pudens*.

Next to the discoveries which have been made, and are still being prosecuted, on the Palatine Hill, in the old Palace of the Cæsars, no explorations have, in recent times, been of deeper value to the Bible student than those which are believed to have led to the identification of the House of CLEMENS, St Paul's fellow-labourer, "whose name is in the Book of Life" (Phil. iv. 3). This illustrious convert was of royal blood, member of the noble family of the Anicii, and in person and character described by one of the Fathers of the second century, as "a man replete with all knowledge, and most skilful in the liberal

House of Clemens.

arts." While yet a boy of twelve years of age, he was consigned, in the absence of his parents at Athens, to the guardianship of tutors in Rome, who nurtured him in "manly studies and virtuous actions." Owing, however, to his speculative turn of mind, he was involved, in early youth, in a severe mental conflict, especially regarding the immortality of the soul and a future life. In vain he betook himself to the varied schools of philosophy; he only felt bewildered amid their sophistries and disputations. He even resorted to the magicians of Alexandria, in hopes that by their arts and incantations they might be able to conjure some human spirit back from the invisible world, to solve the question on which he found the most reputed oracles of earth were dumb. Meanwhile, he heard the tidings that the Son of God had appeared in Judea. He listened to the glorious revelations of the Prophet of Galilee, from the lips of His servants in the Roman capital. His doubts were resolved; he embraced the truth as it is in Jesus with heroic confidence, and enrolled himself among the number of its faithful witnesses. In these days, when the name has attained an historical celebrity unknown before, it may not be uninteresting to add, that he is credited as having been the first bearer of the 'glad tidings' to the city of Metz, which then in importance and population was one of the chief towns of France. We have good reason to believe from Eusebius, Origen, and Jerome, that he became afterwards Bishop of Rome. Trajan, becoming jealous of his increasing influence, banished him to the Chersonesus, where, degraded to the condition of a slave, with a brand on his forehead, and subjected to cruel infamy and dishonour, he was compelled to work in the mines and marble quarries. At length his name was added to the noble army of martyrs; for with an anchor round his neck, he was thrown into the sea, though the body was said subsequently to be discovered and interred in Rome.*

Under the guidance of the Prior of the Con-
Recent excavations. vent of St Clemente, to whom I had an obliging letter of introduction, I was enabled to explore the very interesting substructions, which, altogether owing to his zeal and enthusiasm, have been brought to light; and I would here desire to make, in passing, grateful acknowledgment of his courtesy and kindness.

Church of St Clemente. For long the Church of St Clemente was considered one of the most venerable in Rome, dating at all events from the twelfth century. It is situated on the slope of the Cœlian hill, between St John Lateran and the Coliseum, and possesses much still in its interior to gratify the lover of ancient ecclesi-

---

* We may give the following as a specimen of the credulity of the age (although in this case the myth must be allowed to be a beautiful one), that angels constructed a tomb and built a Church over it in the depths of the sea, where the martyr's body fell ; and that year by year, on the anniversary of his death, the waves receded to permit the faithful to visit his sepulchre !

astical architecture. I may particularise its Atrium, surmounted with a Gothic canopy of the thirteenth century; its unique choir in front of the tribune, encircled with a balustrade of white marble, flanked by two quaint pulpits or 'ambones;' its handsome candelabrum in Mosaic; its pavement studded with fragments of green porphyry; the strange picture on the vault of the tribune, containing a representation of the four rivers flowing in paradise; and among other symbols in this latter, that oldest and most remarkable one (met with also several times in the Catacombs), of the Peacock, as the emblem of Immortality. From the incongruities in the style, as well as from the careless way in which portions of the more elaborate work are put together, the eye of the experienced archæologist or architect at once discerns, that the existing building must have been indebted to some other edifice or edifices for much that is most valuable. Accordingly, the interest attaching to it has been considerably superseded by the discovery made of a still older Church below, which very possibly may have been despoiled of many of its adornments, and especially of its beautiful choir, to enrich the newer Basilica built in later times above it. The carvings and inscriptions, and specially the marvellous number of frescoes, throw much valuable light on the Christianity of the earlier centuries. The cause of the discovery may be stated in a few words. As the Prior, thirteen years ago, was engaged in making some repairs in the contiguous convent, he came upon a wall covered with some pictures, which induced him to prosecute his researches; these led to the disclosure of an ancient edifice resting on massive stonework. He has succeeded in clearing out the two aisles and nave, and tracing the line of pillars which supported the roof. We approached this singular subterranean Basilica with lighted tapers, by a flight of steps leading from the sacristy of the upper building, a depth of twenty feet. It would be entirely out of

Older Basilica.

place here to enter into a further detail of this interesting edifice* with its crude works of art, paintings, inscriptions, sculptures, and precious marbles. The absence of the nimbus round the heads of the sacred figures in the frescoes, is itself a remarkable indication of antiquity,— that symbol never being employed by the earlier painters. But the portion which possessed the deepest interest to me, was that in connection with the supposed discovery of the "House" or "Oratory" of St Paul's fellow-labourer; *House of Clemens.* the very Oratory which he was reputed by tradition to have "built in his own palace at the foot of the Cœlian," and where the young catechumens were in the habit of repairing for instruction in the mysteries of the faith. It is well known that during the first three centuries, Christians were forbidden, on their own account, to erect Churches; their

---

* A full and interesting account of these discoveries will be found in "St Clement and his Basilica in Rome," by Rev. Joseph Mulhooly. Rome, 1869. Also see Murray's excellent "Handbook of Modern Rome."

assemblages for worship and communion took place in private, in the larger houses belonging to their brethren. If, therefore, the identification of this vaulted chamber be correct (and we have the strongest reason to believe that it is so), then it must have been the dwelling in which the early disciples were in the habit of assembling: nay, after being released from his first imprisonment, where St Paul himself, along with Barnabas, Luke, Aristarchus, and others, may have, more than once, met to speak of the things of the kingdom, and to commemorate together their Lord's dying love in His own memorial rite. Moreover, after the establishment of the Christian religion under Constantine, it is very natural to suppose that the original dimensions of the Oratory would be extended, until they embraced the Basilica which has recently been excavated. The approach to it is along a wall formed of enormous blocks of volcanic tufa, indicating a very early period, antecedent to the Christian era; indeed,

supposed by some to be as old as the times of
Servius Tullius. We could trace in rude characters, on several of the recently-exhumed
frescoes, the name of the imperial convert.
The House or Oratory itself has an arched roof,
symmetrical in its structure, and composed of
richly-carved square stones. The only anomaly
in connection with it, and one which has given
rise to considerable discussion among antiquarians, is the discovery of a small Temple of
Mythras, with a Pagan altar of marble in the
centre, in which is a bas-relief of Mythra sacri-
ficing a bull. But there are ingenious and satisfactory explanations regarding this proximity of
the heathen shrine, which we need not here particularise, but which go far to refute any objec-
tions to the accepted theory of the adjoining
chamber having been the veritable house of
so distinguished a member and ornament of the
early Church. It may only further be added,
that the supposed remains of Clement, also the
few bones said to have been left by the lions

who were let loose in the neighbouring amphitheatre on the martyred Ignatius, have been interred in a beautiful tomb and shrine, situated immediately under the altar of the upper Church.

Having thus explored with deep interest the House of Clement, I was desirous of having a similar gratification with regard to that of another of St Paul's reputed converts, of whose name he also makes honourable mention (2 Tim. iv. 21), I mean that of PUDENS. The story of Pudens has a peculiar interest to us. He seems to have been the son of a Roman senator, sent by the Emperor Claudius to be Governor of the Regni—the southern province of England, embracing Surrey and Sussex. While there, he sought in marriage the hand of the daughter of a British King (some say Cogidubnus, some Caractacus), a beautiful young Princess of the age of seventeen, who, in the meantime, was sent to Rome. In order to obviate

House of Pudens,

any bar to marriage with a foreigner (one, too, who probably occupied the position of a hostage at the Imperial Court), Pudens, on returning himself to the capital, requested the Emperor—his imperial patron—to adopt her in the first instance as his daughter, and to bestow upon her, from his own name, that of CLAUDIA. Claudia had already become a Christian, under the teaching and influence probably of a noble matron, Pomponia Græcina, whose husband, Aulus Plautius, had lately been in command of the invading Roman army. After being resident for some time in the capital, the union took place of the Island Princess with the Christian Senator, whose names are thus appropriately found conjoined in St Paul's concluding salutation in his Second Epistle to Timothy,—"*Pudens*, and *Linus*, and *Claudia:*" indicating the interesting fact, that during his last imprisonment, when others less courageous were deterred from crossing his dungeon, he was visited there by the daughter of a British King.

and Claudia.

Regarding the character of *Pudens*, the influence for good he exerted in the early Church, or his special connection with St Paul in the city of their common residence, we know nothing. He would seem to have had the art of conciliating foes, as well as retaining friends. We find Martial, the poet, informing him that he "would dedicate no more verses to him, seeing he had changed his religion." Notwithstanding this threat of alienation, however, they had lived and died with their friendship unbroken; for the poet dedicates an ode on the birth of his first child, and subsequently wrote a lament on his death. Through his matrimonial alliance, it is curious to know that this Roman patrician was the possessor of land in the southern counties of England; for in making excavations in the town of Chichester in 1723, a Roman inscription was discovered, on which it is expressly stated that the site of a temple, erected by a guild of carpenters or smiths, dedicated to Neptune and

Minerva, by the authority of the Imperial Legate, was "granted free" by *Pudens, the son of Pudentius.**

He had two daughters, Pudentiana and Praxedes,† the former of whom, by means of the Church which bears her name, has done more than anything else to perpetuate her father's memory.

---

* See an interesting Treatise, entitled "Claudia and Pudens." By Archdeacon Williams. 1848. The inscription is now preserved in a summer-house in the gardens of Goodwood, and is as follows,—the letters that are wanting being conjecturally supplied :—

"[N]eptuni et Minervæ templum
[Pr]o salute d[omu]s divinæ
[ex] auctoritat [e Tib.] Claud.
[Co]gidubni r. leg. aug. in Brit.
[Colle]gium fabror. et qui in eo,
[a sacris] sunt d s. d d nante aream
[Pud]ente Pudentini fil."

See too Alford's "*Excursus on Pudens and Claudia*," Greek Test., vol. iii., Proleg., pp. 104, 105, where it is surmised that "Pudens may possibly have been attached in capacity of adjutant to King Cogidubnus, and that his presentation of an area for a temple to Neptune and Minerva may have been occasioned by escape from shipwreck, the college of carpenters (shipbuilders) being commissioned to build it to their patrons, Neptune and Minerva." P. 104.

† I did not see the Church erected to the latter, but I believe it possesses valuable mosaics.

The Church of St Pudentiana, now in connection with a Bernardine Convent, is built on the Viminal Hill, not far from Santa Maria Maggiore. It is in one respect even of greater interest than St Clemente, from its undoubted antiquity, being the Mother Church of Rome, the primitive Cathedral of the metropolis, possibly, indeed, of Christendom. It was built (or perhaps more accurately, as we shall immediately note, enlarged and extended) by Pope Pius I., A.D. 141, on the site of the "House of Pudens." The Church itself is rich in mosaics, dating, according to some, from the ninth, according to others, from the fourth century. It is said to contain in a deep well (although this is exceedingly doubtful) the bones of three thousand martyrs. In the roof of the beautiful side chapel of the Cætanis, though of a much later date, amid other decorations well worthy of note, is a singular mosaic, representing the daughters of the Christian Senator collecting by sponges into a golden vase or urn,

Church of St Pudentiana.

the blood of some of these faithful witnesses. In the apse, at the extreme end, opposite the entrance door, and immediately above the altar, is a similar picture. It exhibits Christ enthroned, with the Apostles Paul and Peter on either side, and the two daughters of Pudens holding in their hands a crown of martyrdom. These devoted women, who in childhood and youth may have enjoyed the prayers, or listened to the counsels of the great Apostle, seem to have led lives of loftiest self-sacrifice and consecration. The great wealth bequeathed to them on the decease of their parents and their brother, was freely dedicated to the service of Christ, and to supply the needs of their poorer brethren. During the first great persecution they braved every insult and danger for the sake of the truth and its defenders, personally ministering to those who were in prison and in chains, bringing the tortured and mutilated to their own home on the Viminal, binding up their wounds, and with their own hands shrouding the martyrs who had been denied the rites of burial by their murderers.

I was specially desirous, in visiting this Church, of obtaining access (in which there is some difficulty) to the recent excavations. I was fortunate enough, accidentally, to meet at the entrance Mr P——, whose archæological enthusiasm, and his willingness to impart his discoveries to others, are in keeping with that of the Prior in the sister Church of St Clemente. It was by his own unaided efforts, after considerable difficulties with the Papal authorities, the excavations were carried out, and the interesting subterranean edifice brought to light. In his company I was enabled most satisfactorily and intelligently to explore these strange substructions. The mere substructions themselves cannot be compared in art-interest and variety of detail with those of St Clemente;—the most conspicuous are a bath-room; one chamber with a spacious archway; and another, on a lower level still, with

Recent Excavations.

vaulted roof and mosaic pavement of the first century. To these may be added some underground passages, including the unmistakable cellars, where, in former days, were stored the "Amphoræ" of this old Patrician Palace. But there was a profound interest, too, in these damp, dripping, lonely vaults. After the old Roman Senator and Christian was in his grave, doubtless the Faithful would take refuge there, and, under the protection of those who inherited his name and his faith, utilise them as places of worship, when they dared not with safety meet in the Basilica above. In this other "Church in the House," therefore, as in the case of St Clemente, one could in thought retrace the past, and imagine the days *Associations with the House of Pudens.* when, within these very inclosures, the prayer was uttered, the hymn sung, the word of counsel and comfort imparted, the bread of everlasting life (the blessed emblem and memorial) broken: the hands of gentle love and tenderness, in whose veins flowed the blood of the Cæsars, washing stripes, binding up wounds, wiping away tears, whispering into the dull ear of the scourged and tortured and dying, hopes "full of immortality"—composing their limbs in the last long sleep—an unseen but present Saviour rehearsing doubtless His own words :—" I was a stranger, and ye took me in: naked, and ye clothed me: I was sick, and ye visited me: I was in prison, and ye came unto me" (Matt. xxv. 35). But such sacred associations were by no means confined to these underground places of concealment. That upper Church has this additional interest attached to it, over and above that of St Clemente, that it may not only have been built on the site of Pudens' House, but (in a less amplified shape, perhaps) may have originally formed the very Basilica of his Palace. These Basilicas, attached to every great Roman mansion (as graphically described to us by our conductor), were equivalent to the Barons' halls of olden times in England, where assemblages took place of retainers and vassals. The name, originally thus applied to Roman dwellings, came to be transferred to the Christian Church. Not only so, but when, on the establishment of the Christian religion in the Roman Empire under Constantine, the erection of ecclesiastical fabrics was sanctioned and encouraged, the shape of the Basilica was retained, as being most convenient in form, alike for conducting worship and accommodating worshippers. It is interesting for us, then, to think, that during the reign of Nero, this same hall of a Roman Senator, who had espoused the faith of Christ, may have had its doors opened to receive the handful of infant believers in the City of the Cæsars. Many of those whose names are mentioned in the closing chapter of Romans, may have listened in that very spot to the words of eternal life, and taken sweet counsel together; nay, as our reliable guide observed, as we passed over the pavement with its portions of ancient mosaic, "St Paul himself may possibly have been here." *

---

* Among the other relics shown, is the half of the com-

But I pass to another locality which has its own special memories in connection with St Paul in Rome. The most interesting hours spent in the old capital were among the excavations of the Palace of the Cæsars, on the Palatine Hill. These, as is well-known, were commenced many years ago, under the auspices of Napoleon III., and are still vigorously prosecuted by the Italian Government. Among the other ruins and substructions already disclosed, there is one which, from its more than probable association with the closing scenes in the life of the Great Apostle, specially arrested attention; I mean, that which is known as the "*Basilica Jovis.*"

Basilica on the Palatine.

We have just been describing, in connection with the house of Pudens and Clement, the Basilica which formed an invariable adjunct

---

munion-table said to have been used by St Paul; the other half being shown in St John Lateran. The legend, we need not say, is utterly unreliable; but it is interesting even to note this traditional connection of the name of the Apostle with the Basilica of his illustrious convert.

to the larger dwellings of the more illustrious citizens. A similar Hall, only on a more imposing scale, adjoined the Imperial Palace on the Palatine. Moreover, the latter was more particularly used as a court of justice, where, in the presence either of the Emperor or his legate, trials took place and political appeals were heard. It was, indeed, from these regal Basilicas, more than from the lesser private ones, that the form of future ecclesiastical places of worship, to which reference has just been made, was taken,—the tribune at one end, and the double row of columns running up on either side, forming a central nave and two aisles. The design was at once simple and imposing. It is certainly historically curious, (we may be forgiven the repetition) that a Pagan court of justice should thus have given architectural shape to thousands of Christian Churches; this being specially the case with regard to Rome itself, where the oblong or rectangular type is almost universal, culminating in the Great Basilica of St Peter's itself.*

While standing on that pavement of marble on the northern summit of the hill overlooking the Forum and the Arch of Titus, the question is naturally suggested — If this be the Basilica of the Imperial Palace, can it be, or rather, can it fail to be, the spot where Paul stood eighteen hundred years ago, prosecuting his "appeal unto Cæsar," and where he probably confronted, at all events at his first trial, the Emperor himself? If the opinion of some archæological authorities be correct, viz., that the Basilica discovered is of the age of Domitian, then, of course, these pavements and fragmentary columns could not have belonged to the judiciary tribunal before which the Apostle pleaded his cause. But I venture the

The probable scene of St Paul's trial.

---

* So remarkable is this uniformity of the Basilica type in the Roman places of worship, that it becomes a positive relief and refreshment to the eye to gaze once more on the interiors of the Gothic Cathedrals and Churches of the North and West.

assertion on the authority of one whose testimony is worthy of all credit, that if we are forced to surrender the claims of this precise building as belonging to the Pauline age, we may feel the strong certainty, at all events, that it occupies the very same position with the Court where the Apostle stood, though possibly on a lower level. Because, although the *building* itself from time to time, whether under Domitian or Vespasian, might undergo alteration, there was no great likelihood of any such in the site. Moreover, the form and construction of the Court itself was equally stereotyped and unchanging.

We felt therefore, in gazing upon it, making every allowance for uncertainty, how fully we could realise the actual scene on the two successive occasions in which "the Ambassador in bonds" was sisted before a human judge and judgment-seat. At the farther end, where that semicircular wall incloses the building, and elevated into a platform some five feet above the pavement, was the *subsellia*, where sat the judges, twenty in number, and these generally of Prætorian dignity; that central seat or throne (the "curule chair," though it has no traces left of its inlay of gold and ivory) was reserved for the Emperor or his consular legate. The capricious monarch, in terms of the Roman constitution, acting as chief magistrate, frequently gave his personal presidency, wearing the imperial purple and surrounded by Lictors with their fasces; but in doing so, he was as frequently in the habit of ignoring the judicial wisdom of his assessors, and exercising the most absolute and despotic authority.* Underneath this raised bench or tribune were ranged the subservient lawyers. Near that circular stone of Egyptian porphyry and granite in front of the tribune, stood an altar, on which the robed Senators laid their hands, and swore to judge righteous judgment. A few paces farther back, where there are still the remains

---

* See Josephus, xx. 8-11.

of a richly-wrought bar of marble, would stand the Apostle, chained by the arm to one of the Prætorian Guards, while his prosecutors would be seated near. There would be room also left for any advocate or advocates, who might be present to render assistance in pleading his cause. In his case we know there were none—"No man stood with me" (2 Tim. iv. 16). The illustrious Confessor was left unaided to answer the successive counts or indictments. ONE Intercessor alone, mightier than the Cæsars, was invisibly at his side: "Notwithstanding *the Lord* stood with me, and strengthened me" (2 Tim. iv. 17). We may be sure that he who had so often appeared undaunted before the delegates of the imperial throne, did not quail when he was at last confronted with their master. "To him all the majesty of Roman despotism was nothing more than an empty pageant;—the imperial demigod himself was but one of the princes of this world that come to nought. Thus would he stand calm and collected, ready to answer the charges of his accusers, and knowing that, in the hour of his need, it should be given him what to speak."* So many of the public, to whom the comparatively limited space could afford admission, would occupy the vacant space in the nave and aisles. Among these, on the present occasion, we may include exasperated Jews from Palestine,† Ephesus, and Greece; hating Gentiles;‡ as well as the few friends who dared thus venture on perilous ground to wait the result of the pleadings; while the surmise has been made (I believe by De Rossi) regarding one of three lower platforms outside, which have been uncovered in the course of the excavations, that

---

* Howson and Conybeare, vol. ii. p. 457.

† Josephus informs us that Ishmael the High Priest, accompanied by the "chief men" from Jerusalem, was in Rome in the year A.D. 61. A quarrel about the building of a wall was the ostensible reason,—the true one seems rather to point to the prosecution of their vengeance against the turbulent ringleader, their formidable adversary now on his trial.

‡ "So that all the Gentiles might hear" (2 Tim. iv. 17), indicating a large assemblage.

from it the verdict of the imperial tribunal was communicated, in cases of interest, to the crowd assembled below.

We can only further imagine the close of the trial. The verdict of each assessor was written on a tablet, and these collected were compared by the presiding judge. In the case of the Apostle, the momentous and decisive Latin word, CONDEMNO, uttered by the imperial delegate, would ring through the pillared hall and breathless audience, and perhaps thereafter be proclaimed to the multitude gathered beneath at the entrance to the Forum. He is now "ready to be offered," and the time of his departure is at hand.

There is always a halo of interest surrounding the place associated with the closing hours of an illustrious man—the spot which witnessed the sun of a noble life hasting to its setting. Among other localities connected with St Paul's Roman residence, we surely may *The Mamertine Dungeon.*

inquire, with pardonable curiosity, regarding the dungeon to which he was remanded, probably for many months after his second trial; where, it may be, after the sentence of death was pronounced, he had his last touching interview with his dearest friends, and among these Pudens and Claudia;—where that affecting final letter was penned to his son Timothy, overflowing as it is alike with fidelity and affection;—the spot where the great champion, feeling that the long battle was over, could ungird his armour and say, "I have fought the good fight."

It was with these thoughts uppermost, that I paid my first visit to "the Mamertine dungeon." Like other venerable relics of ancient Rome, it has given rise to an amicable war of opinion. But like not a few such disputed localities, as we shall presently find, it has had new and important light within a recent period, indeed within a few months, thrown on it.

For long a dungeon has been exhibited at the

foot of the descent from the Capitol, below the small Church of S. Giuseppe dei Fal-egnami, close to the entrance to the Forum, and beside the Arch of Septimius Severus. It consists of two chambers. My first exploration was under the torch-guidance of one of the ordinary ecclesiastic officials (never very satisfactory when you can have a better), who retailed the old baseless traditions, given by Baronius, of the impress of St Peter's head on the wall—the pillar to which he and St Paul were bound for the space of nine months—and the fountain which miraculously burst forth to supply water for the baptism of the two gaolers, Processus and Martianus, with forty-seven other converted fellow-captives.* The dungeon itself is of undoubted antiquity ; indeed, "one of the few monuments of the kingly period, built in the most massive style of Etruscan architecture, begun by Ancus Martius, and enlarged by Ser-

Traditional Prison of St Paul.

---

* This same fountain, on the authority of Plutarch, is as old as the days of Jugurtha !

vius Tullius, from whom it took the name of Tullian."* It consists of two chambers, an upper and a lower (the upper is the older of the two), constructed of huge blocks of tufa, without cement, fastened together with iron rivets. One side of the lower chamber is excavated from the solid rock. There is a hole in the centre of the floor of the former, from which condemned prisoners were let down to await or undergo their fate. There can hardly be a doubt that these were the dungeons so accurately depicted by Livy as adjoining the Forum ("imminens Foro"). In the lower one, among a list of other victims, the miserable Jugurtha, King of Mauritania, was left to perish by starvation. It is thus circumstantially described by Sallust, in his account of the execution of Cataline's conspirators :—" In the prison called Tertullian, there is a place about ten feet deep, when you have descended a little to the left ; it is surrounded on the sides by walls, and is

---
* Murray *in loco*.

closed above by a vaulted roof of stone. The appearance of it, from the filth, the darkness, and the smell, is terrific."*

Such is the dungeon which has long been associated in Christian legend with the last scenes in the life of St Peter and St Paul. In commemoration of their imprisonment, deputies from all the Churches in Rome assemble by torch-light on the night of the 4th of July, and in solemn silence kneel in front of the traditional pillar. † While the antiquity of the cells, at present exhibited, is indisputable, a twofold reason militates against their being accepted as the place of the Apostle's captivity. The first is, that they were reserved for state prisoners; and it is more than doubtful if "the Missionary of the new religion" would be included under that cate-

Difficulties in accepting it as such, stated.

---

* See this and other details in Murray.

† It will be observed that I have carefully abstained from entering on the vexed historical question of St Peter's alleged residence, imprisonment, and martyrdom at Rome, as not falling within the scope of this volume.

gory; the second, that if there were no such restriction, and we are to consider them as the public prisons of Rome, their size would be manifestly inadequate for the criminal requirements of so vast a population. The question occurs—Could this cell of Tullian, and its still older adjunct, possibly not be only the outer portion or vestibule of a more extensive range of wards which the ardour and patience of the antiquary might yet discover? This is precisely the problem which, we believe, as we now write, is in process of solution, if, indeed, the solution is not already made. And here the public are again indebted to the singular enthusiasm and discernment of the President of the Roman Archæological Society. It was my privilege to accompany him, shortly before leaving Rome, along with other friends, to a newly-discovered range of dungeons, in close proximity with the traditional Mamertine. Passing through a narrow street or lane, amid bales of unsightly goods — the most

Probable solution.

musty of merchandise—we descended by a stair into a spacious subterranean cellar, now converted into a wine-vault, and which is connected with a series of others. There is a large circular aperture in the roof of the principal one, by which, it may be confidently surmised, prisoners, as well as their food, must in ancient times have been lowered; and which in addition might serve for ventilation. The side walls are composed, as in the case of the present Tullian, of large blocks of volcanic tufa. The belief of the discoverer of these spacious substructions is, that they will be found to be the veritable wards or cells of the Great Prison, of which the one now exhibited formed a small integral portion. Indeed, he had succeeded in discovering a narrow passage (partially cleared when I saw it, for several yards) leading from the lower Mamertine, and which (by continuing still further the removal of the débris and rubbish which fills it up) may probably lead to an outlet in some of those grim wine-vaults we had just explored. If his theory be correct, it may serve so far to demolish the old traditional association with the more limited dungeon below the Church of S. Giuseppe; but it would remove other difficulties; and in doing so would strengthen and confirm the belief that some one or other, at all events, of these gloomy underground cells must have been the place where the great Apostle bequeathed his dying testimony to the Church in all ages. We shall wait with interest the result of the excavations.

If the scene of St Paul's last imprisonment have its mournful interest, so surely must that of his martyrdom.* The worthless miracles which superstition and credulity have clustered around the reputed site are to be rejected without examination.

The Scene of St Paul's Martyrdom.

---

* Owing to his Roman citizenship, he was happily saved the horrors of the Amphitheatre, and the ignominy and torture of crucifixion. We are far from sure that he equally escaped the preliminary scourging by lictors rods, inflicted on those condemned to capital punishment.

But on reaching these gentle swells in the Campagna some three miles from the Ostian Gate, and which have long been marked by the Church of the 'Tre Fontane,' I had every reason to believe I was treading the spot where the Church on earth was called to mourn the greatest of her losses, and where the Church in heaven had added to her roll the most illustrious name in her noble army of martyrs. Amid the confusing network of Roman streets, and the changes to which the city's crowded localities were subject, there might be more ground for hesitancy and debate regarding the precise position of the "lodging" and "hired house;" but the place of execution—one of the Tyburns of ancient Rome*—was not liable to such shiftings and vicissitudes. Besides, we may feel assured

---

* This may not indeed have been the ordinary place of execution, or that in most frequent use. It may possibly rather have been the spot where capital punishment was inflicted in cases when, on account of sympathy with the prisoner, or the cause for which he suffered, publicity was to be avoided within the city itself.

the Faithful would not thus readily let go their recollection of what was invested with such sad yet glorious memories of suffering and triumph, —" the holiest spot in God's acre." The excursion to Aqua Salvia is not in itself an interesting one, so far as either ancient remains or modern surroundings are concerned, if we except the Temple of Vesta, and the recently-discovered " Marmorata." The base of the old Aventine Hill is skirted on the left, and more than one near glimpse to the right is obtained of " the yellow Tiber," with its mud banks ; not rendered more picturesque, as we passed, by the recent calamitous inundations. The building which most deeply arrests on the way, alike from its own singularity and antiquity, is the Pyramid of Caius Cestius, close by the old Ostian Gate.* It possesses, moreover, this additional interest, that it was there when the unresisting prisoner was hurried by, under a sultry sun in the end of June, to the place of his exe-

---

* See Engraving, p. 100.

cution; so that, as it has been well said, "Among the works of man, that Pyramid is the only surviving witness of Paul's martyrdom."—(*Howson and Conybeare.*) In passing along the straight road (probably, too, unchanged since the first century), and which still con- *Chapel of the two Apostles.* ducts to Ostia, the student interested in tracing the footsteps of the great Apostle, cannot resist pausing for a moment by the small inconspicuous chapel on the wayside, to mark one of the scenes which tradition, although without any authority, has grafted on this memorable last journey. In the rude bas-relief above the door, is a slab containing a representation of the supposed parting which here took place between St Peter and St Paul. The words alleged to have been spoken at this farewell interchange of affection, have as singular a quaintness about them as the sculptures they illustrate.

" And St Paul said to St Peter, Peace be with thee, Foundation of the Church, Shepherd of the flock of Christ."

F

"And Peter said to Paul, Go in peace, Preacher of good tidings, and Guide of the salvation of the just."

We may adopt the safe verdict of Dr Cave, the earliest English biographer of both Apostles (1676), that however fictitious may be this and other recorded incidents, "the best is, which of them soever started first, they both came at last to the same end of the race; to those palms and crowns which are reserved for all good men in heaven."

A little further on—if we may venture to refer to the one other legend connected with the martyrdom—Plautilla, a Christian matron and convert, placed herself by the wayside as the mournful crowd approached. She was desirous of obtaining a last look of the Apostle. She knelt as he passed, and with many tears besought his farewell blessing. The doomed prisoner made a request that she would give him her veil with which to cover his eyes, and that he would faithfully return the loan

Legend of Plautilla.

after death. The boon was granted; and, after his martyrdom, he was said to have appeared to her, and to have restored it stained with his blood.*

Meanwhile, let us enter the Church of Tre Fontane. It is situated several hundred yards to the left of the Ostian road. *Church of Tre Fontane.* But for two churches adjoining, we should have said that it occupies a retired spot. Glimpses are obtained from it of Cavi, the Alban Hills, and the bright villas of Frescati. Imagination could vividly depict the tragic scene of that memorable day, eighteen hundred years ago. Ostia was not the deserted town which comparatively now it is, but one of the two "*Liverpools* of ancient Italy," Puteoli being the other. The road to it, therefore, would not be, as at present, comparatively deserted in winter, and almost totally so in the summer

---

* I recognised this old legend represented in bas-relief on one of the colossal bronze doors in St Peter's, which belonged to the old Basilica. St Paul is represented in the clouds restoring the veil.

months, when the malaria with its pall of death hangs over the blighted soil. It would be busy rather with traders and wayfarers passing to and from the capital and its maritime port. Little would these crowds dream, as they were thus speeding along on their errands of business or pleasure, of all that was connected with that military escort—an unwonted cavalcade of soldiers, and the figure who walked calm and unruffled in their midst; or as, when pausing in that green hollow, they caught, it may be, in the bright sun, the flash of the executioner's sword, which summoned the hero to his crown!

We shall not stop to enumerate the mythical tales and legends which the walls of this little church enshrine. These commemorations of the chisel are as painful and obtrusive in such a place, as are the modern whitewashed walls which surround the olives of Gethsemane. They do not serve in any degree to vivify remembrances, far less to foster hallowed emotion. More impressive far, it appeared to us, would it have been, had the lonely spot remained uncenotaphed, without stone or tree to mark it, allowing the meditative pilgrim himself to recall the reality, and wake up to the feeling, 'Here the great Apostle died.' In entering the church, a modern marble slab on the wall to the right, contains an effective bas-relief representing the swordsman completing his stern duty, and below it an inscription commencing with the words, " Paulo— Gentium—Apostolo." In the right of the transept is the traditional broken pillar, encircled by an iron railing, which formed the block for the executioner; while close by, are the three miraculous fountains, said to have burst forth at each bound as the severed head struck the earth. Over them are erected three altars, with a representation of St Paul in relief.*

---

* The water of the nearest of these fountains is said to be still warm, the second tepid, and the third cold! An archæologist I incidentally met, conversant with Rome, and interested in the subject of my inquiries, mentioned, that four years

One other spot still claims reference, before completing these memories of St Paul in Rome. We naturally pass from the scene of his death to that of his grave.

Place of St Paul's Burial and Tomb.

Whatever were the superstitious abuses to which the custom led, it was, we know, the habit of the Primitive Church most sacredly to guard the spot where martyr-blood was shed. St Cyprian is the interpreter, in a single sentence, of the sentiment of the faithful in these ages: "To the bodies of those who depart by the outlet of a glorious death, let a more zealous watchfulness be given." Can we believe

---

ago, when visiting the Church of the Tre Fontane, he had the curiosity to measure the respective distances between the reputed pillar of martyrdom and the three miraculous fountains. It was exactly seven feet. He mentioned further, that though rejecting the tradition as utterly baseless, it was yet *possible* that a head could have made three such bounds after decapitation. In returning, however, recently to the same place, he found that the distance between these altars, over the reputed fountains, had been considerably and unscrupulously widened, so as better to suit architectural symmetry. Such is the versatility with which Rome can accommodate facts to æsthetic and other requirements!

that those who mingled in that weeping crowd on the Ostian way, would fail to secure for the mangled remains a loving burial? that those, in the same or in a subsequent age, who, by means of rude sarcophagi and inscriptions in the vaults of the Catacombs, took such pains to mark the dormitory of their sainted dead, would omit rearing a befitting memorial in the case of their illustrious spiritual chief? "The grave of St Paul," says Chrysostom, "is well known" (Hom. in Heb. xxvi.); and the assertion of this eminent Father had an augmented meaning in after ages, in the many thousands of pilgrims from all lands who flocked to the reputed shrine of the great Apostle. I can truly say, that independent altogether of its associations with this devoted servant of his Lord, no Church in that city of churches (not even St Peter's itself) so impressed me, as did this magnificent ecclesiastical monument, San Paolo-fuori-le-mura. It is situated nearly half-way between the Pyramid of Cestius

San Paolo-fuori-le-mura.

and the Tre Fontane. It has no fascination, rather the reverse, in its outward architecture; but its interior consists of a vast Basilica, with a row of eighty Corinthian columns (monoliths) of polished granite. These were the gift of the Catholic sovereigns and princes of Europe, and are reflected, as in a sea of glass, in the floor of the nave and aisles. The original Church was built by the Emperor Constantine, A.D. 388, over the garden and cemetery, or rather catacomb, of a wealthy Roman matron converted to Christianity, named Lucina.* The building was enlarged under

---

* It was in this same Catacomb of St Lucina that Boldetti discovered an inscription remarkable for its antiquity. The accuracy of the date he assigned it (in the age of the Flavian Emperors, end of first century, and consequently about forty years after the interment of St Paul) has been confirmed by De Rossi. The translation on the slab is as follows :—" As a resting-place for Titus Flavius Eutychius, who lived nineteen years, eleven months, three days, his dearest friend, Marcus Orbius, gave this spot. Farewell, beloved." It is surmised that the Catacomb may have been commenced as a place of Christian sepulture immediately after receiving the body of St Paul.—*See Northcote's "Roma Sotteranea,"* 1869.

successive Emperors, and attained great splendour under the Pontificate of Leo III. in the eighth century, when it had nearly double the number of its present columns, with mosaics, and altars of rare workmanship. It possessed this additional interest to the British visitor, that as the Church of St John Lateran was under the special guardianship of France, so that of St Paolo, previous to the Reformation, claimed as its protectors the sovereigns of England. A calamitous fire in 1823 reduced the beautiful pile almost to ashes. Among the few portions of value which escaped the ravages of the flames, were the mosaics of the thirteenth century on the western façade, and on the vaults of the Tribune. In the frontispiece to this volume, although the colouring is intransferable, we give the gorgeous baldacchino which occupies the space between the transept and the nave, supported on four pillars of red oriental alabaster, with their gilded capitals and Gothic canopy. It surmounts the traditional tomb of the Apostle, and bears the superscription :—

"TU ES VAS ELECTIONIS, SANCTE PAULE APOSTOLE. PRÆDICATOR VERITAS. IN UNIVERSO MUNDO."

More striking to me than all that costly splendour,—more impressive even, had I seen it, than the hidden silver sarcophagus, surmounted with a golden cross of a hundred and fifty pounds weight,—were the Apostle's own simple words. They seemed silently to suggest with what a sublime indifference, compared to nobler verities, he would have looked around on all that cold magnificence—

"MIHI VIVERE CHRISTUS EST, ET MORI LUCRUM."

In gazing on the Apostle's tomb, one other feature could not fail to arrest. In immediate *Reputed Tomb of Timothy.* juxtaposition with it, in front of the high altar, is a shrine of more modest pretensions, on which is inscribed the one name, which tells it own touching story—

"TIMOTHEI."

Here the ashes of the Apostle Timothy are

said to rest. Strong is the temptation, for once, not too exactingly to demand or scrutinise authority for the truth of a legend in itself so beautiful, that these two honoured servants of Christ, who had loved and laboured, wept and prayed, sorrowed and rejoiced together, are now resting side by side, a true "family burying-place," the father and his "own son in the faith."*

---

* The last remembrance I have of that magnificent Basilica and its sepulchre, is not a pleasing one, and too faithfully attests the unchanged spirit and principles of the Papal Church. A friend had distributed, among the soldiers outside (who had gratefully accepted the boon), a few tracts, embodying simple truths, such as St Paul would have loved to inculcate; and which, moreover, could not have injured, in the remotest degree, the susceptibilities of the most fastidious ecclesiasticism. They were seized by the priest, who brought them to where I was standing at the tomb of the Apostle, and burnt them at the lamps which surround his shrine. It would have been alike unavailing and perilous, in such a place, to have ventured to remonstrate. I remembered the pillar in St Paul's house in the Via Lata, the vase of blood, and the pendant fetter. *That* is Rome as she was—what she still would be. But I remembered, too, the silent voice in the pillar's inscription. It was Paul's own comment on the futile attempt to insult his ashes, "But the Word of God is not bound!"

After thus exploring, in a visit to Rome, all *Pictures and Statues of St Paul.* that could be seen in connection with the great Apostle, perhaps these introductory remarks would be incomplete, if I did not add a few words from personal observation, regarding any memorials of him there to be seen in sculpture, painting, or medallion. We have it on the authority of Basil, in his Epistle to Julian, that portraits of the Apostles and martyrs existed from Apostolic times; and Ambrose speaks of an authentic portrait of St Paul.* Eusebius informs us that he had seen representations of the Apostles Peter and Paul in paintings. Chrysostom alludes to one which hung in his own chamber; and Augustine mentions "a certain Marcellina, who, in the second century, preserved in her Lararium, among her household gods, the images of Homer, Pythagoras, Jesus Christ, and Paul."† And

---

* See Mr Hemans' interesting work on Roman Antiquities.
† See Mrs Jamieson's "Sacred and Legendary Art." Also Northcote *in loco.*

surely it would be nothing either strange or improbable, that the early converts, who embraced some of the members of wealthy Roman families (living, too, as we have seen, in senatorial palaces), should endeavour to have the face and features of one they so much loved and honoured, perpetuated by the painter's art.

In modern Rome, there is neither picture nor statue of him at all worthy of celebrity; not one which bears the impress of genius, such as the Moses of Michael Angelo in St Pietro in Vinculi, or the grand heads of Jeremiah and Isaiah in the Sistine Chapel by the same great master. It is worthy of note, that in almost all the representations of the Apostle which are to be found in the present day in the city of his martyrdom, whether early, mediæval, or modern, there are these two peculiarities. He is seen with a sword in his hand, sometimes leaning on it, sometimes holding it aloft,—the emblem of that sword of the Spirit with which he fought and conquered. Also, he is almost invariably depicted in conjunction with St Peter; the one as the Apostle of the circumcision sent to the Jews, the other of the uncircumcision—the Apostle of the Gentiles. The two best statues I can recall, are both comparatively modern—the colossal one at the foot of the flight of steps leading to the façade of St Peter's, and another by Girometti adjoining the high altar in the San Paolo; but they are both too conventional, with the Grecian face and drapery. It is curious that the statue nearest to the little Church where the sermons which follow in this volume were delivered, was one of the Apostle, occupying the niche between two Doric columns in the Porta del Popolo; but it is poor, alike in sentiment and execution.

"In the pictures of St Paul, the Greek type is also followed—the long flowing beard, blue tunic, and white mantle."* The oldest one in Rome, of the single figure, was painted on the walls of the Cemetery of Priscilla in the second

---

* Jamieson.

or third century. He is there represented in
the dress of a traveller, with sandalled feet—the
Good Shepherd standing on his right, and the inscription above, "Paulus—Pastor—Apostolus."*
Next in point of age to this, is a mosaic in the
Basilica of Sta Maria Maggiore. It is placed in
the arch which separates the sanctuary from
the nave. In the centre is a throne, with emblems from the Apocalypse, surmounted by a
cross enriched with precious stones, and St Paul
and St Peter on either side. The most valuable
painting of the Apostle, as a mere work of art,
is I believe in the Lateran, which at the time I
was in Rome was closed. The best which came
under my observation, although considerably
damaged, was in the curious old Chapel adjoining the Basilica of St Agnese-fuori-le-mura.
It is a fresco, not by the great Michael Angelo,
but by his illustrious namesake Michael Angelo
Carravaggio. The Apostle is represented in a
contemplative attitude, with a book in one hand

---

* See Bosio, Sott., p. 519.

and the sword, as usual, in the other. I noted a curious mosaic, supposed to be of date the thirteenth century, above the altar in St Clemente, and another painting in the tribune of St Paolo, in a lunette, representing the Apostle as borne by angels to heaven. In former years, among the ecclesiastical pageants which attracted multitudes at Easter to St Peter's, was one at the close of Vespers on Monday. A Canon appeared on a balcony underneath the vast dome, and in sonorous voice announced that what were now exposed to the view of the faithful, were the famous portraits possessed by Pope Sylvester,—portraits which when shown by him to Constantine, were called by the Emperor "those gods named Peter and Paul."* These and other similar pictures are interesting on account of their antiquity: but undoubtedly the noblest delineation of the Apostle ever executed in Rome, or by Italian painter, was that designed for one of the tapestries in the

---

* See Hemans' "Christian Rome," p. 158.

Sistine Chapel, and which has now been for long the property of the British nation. Well has it been said of that great cartoon by no incompetent judge, "The sublimest ideal of embodied eloquence that ever was expressed in art, is Raphael's 'St Paul preaching at Athens.'" *
Yet the same writer, with equal discernment, expresses doubt whether Raphael did well in adopting so violent a departure from the traditional head (which was so much more expressive of the man of toil and care and sorrow, wasted with watchings and fastings), by substituting that of the conventional Jupiter.

The medallions, pictures on ancient glass, drinking vessels, and lamps, though quaint, inartistic, and possessing a uniform type, are more interesting. One of those on glass, and one of the oldest, I copied as carefully as the hurried circumstances would permit from a case in the Library Museum

Medallions, &c.

---

* "Sacred and Legendary Art," p. 226.

of the Vatican. It is reproduced at the end of the preface to this volume. The execution of the picture, whoever may be the unknown limner, is rude, and the eye the most defective part of the face. It seems to be in accordance with other traditional representations — "the head bald, the nose aquiline, and beard graceful." I am unable to decipher the meaning of the emblem above the head. In another similar glass vessel in the same compartment of the Museum, he is depicted surrounded with four scrolls. A copy of a valuable bronze medallion, three inches in diameter, of St Paul and St Peter, also in the Vatican, will be found carefully rendered in one of the engravings of Mrs Jamieson's "Sacred and Legendary Art." It is considered the earliest known representation of the Apostle, probably in the time of the Flavian Emperors. It was discovered by Boldetti in St Domitilla's Cemetery, in the Catacombs of St Calixtus, and is artistically and classically executed. But it is at present in a portion of the Museum to which, when I was in Rome, the public were forbidden access.

And yet, after all, what is the worth of these imaginative representations? what, even had they been more reliable than they are, would have been their intrinsic value, compared with the picture which, with photographic fidelity, the great Apostle has unconsciously given of himself as reflected in his Epistles. Character is the true portrait; the alone enduring frescoes are good words and noble deeds. Chrysostom truly speaks of him as "though only three cubits high, yet tall enough to reach heaven." Great as were his teachings and writings, his life was greater still. He authorises, in one sense (to use the familiar phrase), the copying of his likeness: but thus the sanction runs, "Be ye also followers (copyers, imitators) of me, even as I (or rather, in as far as I) am a follower (a copyer) of Christ" (1 Cor. xi. 1). "Follow me—copy me," as if he had said, "thus far, but no farther." In another

St Paul's true portrait.

place he gives the similar exhortation, when, holding up before the Church, not himself, but that ONE peerless, spotless Life and Example—(the only ideal and realisation of Christian perfection),—using too a word which has the meaning of "intently gazing" (like the intent gaze of a copyist in transferring to canvas or marble some great original)—"Wherefore, holy brethren, partakers of the heavenly calling, CONSIDER . . . *Christ Jesus.*" (Heb. iii. 1).

The Pyramid of Caius Cestius, and the Ostian Gate.

SERMON I.

St Paul's Announcement of his Purpose in Going to Rome.

"I am debtor both to the Greeks, and to the barbarians, both to the wise, and to the unwise. So, as much as in me is, I AM READY (or earnest) TO PREACH THE GOSPEL TO YOU THAT ARE AT ROME ALSO. FOR I AM NOT ASHAMED OF THE GOSPEL OF CHRIST: FOR IT IS THE POWER OF GOD UNTO SALVATION TO EVERY ONE THAT BELIEVETH; to the Jew first, and also to the Greek."—ROM. i. 14-16.

I.

(*Preached at the Porta del Popolo, February* 19, 1871.)

ROM. I. 15, 16.

"I am ready to preach the gospel to you that are at Rome also. For I am not ashamed of the gospel of Christ: for it is the power of God unto salvation to every one that believeth."

THIS is my first Sunday in ROME. And surely no words could more appropriately inaugurate our services here, than those I have just read as a text. They are the noble testimony of one, whose work has its most sacred associations in this imperial city. I have followed the steps of the great Apostle in other places, consecrated by his name and labours. In Jerusalem, the scene of his youth and early manhood. In approaching Damascus, at the traditional spot of his conversion, and in "the street called Straight," where his rayless eyes and blinded soul received their natural and spiritual vision. On the heights of Mars' Hill where he confronted the polished Athenians. Among the mounds and marshes of Ephesus, now a chaos of ruins—but where, in the zenith of its glory, and under the shadow of Diana's Temple, he unfolded the Truth as it is in Jesus. Finally, along the pathway of the Great Sea, and on "the Island called Melita," when he was pursuing his journey hither, to prosecute and terminate the world-wide commission, " Go thy way, for thou art a chosen vessel unto Me, to bear My name among the Gentiles and kings, and the children of Israel." It is my privilege now to visit the place which listened to his latest testimony, when he was "such an one as Paul the aged;" on whose temples and towers was shed the last gleam of a glorious life. In subsequent Sabbaths, we shall hope, with God's gracious help and blessing, to follow out these varied and interesting memories of St Paul—in his sojourn, labours, sufferings, and death in this old metropolis.

In the words before us, we have the resolution formed by him in the prospect of setting his foot within its gates. They bring before us, in a single verse, the theme which, throughout his long life of sacrifice and consecration, is ever uppermost in his soul,—the glorious Gospel of Christ, aye, Christ Himself, "the Power of God." From the moment he was struck down, in that hour of mighty surrender, when he cried, " Lord, what wouldst Thou have me to do?" till the last breathing of his lips, " I am now ready to be offered, and the time of my departure is at hand," we may say he had but one central thought, around which all others constellated: Jesus was with him first, last, foremost, midmost, upmost, and without end. Wherever he went, that theme was the same: to the astute philosophers of the Areopagus; to the uncultured peasantry in the wilds of Upper Asia; to the Ephesian elders on the sea-beach; to the sailors in the midst of the Adriatic storm; to the mail-clad warriors of this ancient capital. A hundred times over, in the course of his Epistles, is that name mentioned, which is above every name—and the repetition of it seems to impart a new and salient joy and energy to his whole nature. We never hear of him but once in tears, and that once was, when weeping over the enemies of the cross of Him he loved more dearly than all the world beside. Let us, then, as a befitting introduction to subsequent scenes and incidents, listen to the old but never threadworn story, which he announces it to be his purpose to tell once more at Rome ;—the theme of all themes —the power of all powers—the Gospel of the grace of God to dying men and a dying world! In one of his letters written from Rome, this is his watchword and manifesto, "God forbid that I should glory, save in the cross of our Lord Jesus Christ" (Gal. vi. 14). Again, when he intimates his intention of coming to Rome, he says, "And I am sure that, when I come unto you, I shall come in the fulness of the blessing of the Gospel of Christ" (Rom. xv. 29). May we be able, in some lowly measure, to endorse his words.

In the immediately preceding verse, the Apostle announces his purpose, if it be the will of God, to preach "at ROME also;" then he adds "*for*" (and this is the connection of the text)—"for" (although Rome be the world's metropolis) "I am not ashamed to preach even there my loved theme, the Gospel of Christ, "for it is the power of God unto salvation to every one that believeth, to the Jew first, and also to the Greek." Thus we have Romans, Jews, and Greeks,—all specially named and grouped together,—a powerful phalanx of resistance. But this moral hero knew his weapons. He had ranged against him the powers of man; but he was conscious of "a power" mightier than all, and which out of weakness made him strong.

Let us dwell, for a little, on each of the three clauses of our text in succession.

I. "*I am not ashamed of the Gospel of Christ.*"

Now it is at once evident from this assertion, that there was something in that Gospel and its doctrines unpalatable to the wide circle to whom the Apostle wrote and spoke. And we are aware how well-grounded were his fears. The propagators of that Gospel were scorned and vilified as revolutionary fanatics, subverters of the ancient faith, disturbers of the public peace, turning the world upside down. In the words of "the chief of his own nation," who visited him subsequently in his Roman lodging, "As concerning this sect, we know that everywhere it is spoken against." The men might possibly have been tolerated, but their theme was a branded tale. For what was the sum and substance of that theme? Nothing else but this—that the world, the proud world, in the haughty zenith of her glory, should come and lay that glory at the foot of a cross of shame; and confess that, for salvation, its millions were indebted from first to last to a dying Redeemer! Their poets and philosophers and soothsayers had dimly foreshadowed the advent of some great Prince, who was to descend on the earth and inaugurate an era of peace and blessing. Could these dreams possibly have so poor a fulfilment as in the incarnation of the Christ of Nazareth, the son of a lowly woman of Galilee? What! the proud *Roman!* he who subdued kingdoms, stopped the mouths of lions—he who never

imagined any of his heroes could die, far less
die an ignominious death—who dreamt of them,
rather, as translated into palaces of glory or
changed into constellations in the firmament:
how hard for him to take in the truth, that One
mightier than all his gods or demi-gods, the
Saviour of sinners, was a crucified *Man*, who
perished on a felon's cross! And, what was,
perhaps, more insulting than all, that Gospel
(that new religion) was ushered, as in our text,
before the world, by this its apostolic expounder
and interpreter, as "a POWER." "*Power!*"
who dared whisper such a new rival word in
a Roman ear? Was not their whole name and
history and wide empire the embodiment and
apotheosis of Power? What power antagonistic
to his own could a Roman tolerate? Speak to
him of *power*, he would point to the eagles on
his standards, or to the Temple of Victory
crowning one of his seven hills, with its garnered
spoils of vanquished nations. Speak to him of
power, he would point to the subject-empires
over whose broad territories these eagles could
speed for days their unchallenged way without

requiring perch or resting-place. " Thy work, O Roman!" said the greatest of their poets, "is to rule kingdoms."

Again—*The Jew!* Is it possible he can bid farewell to all his revered and time-honoured rites? Is the Temple and all its lofty pageants, the pomp of his solemn feasts, the pride of his ritual, all to pale before the reputed Son of a carpenter? Can he receive as King of the royal nation, a crucified Nazarene? and that, too, when his own law utters the words—"*Cursed is every one that hangeth on a tree?*"

The Greek! Is *he* to part with all his divine philosophy, to accept the teaching and the doctrines of one who perished by a cruel death, among a nation he esteems as *barbarian?* Amid the beautiful dreams of his own mythology, that peopled every wood and grove and stream with a deity, must he say, with St Paul, as he stood amid the splendours of Corinthian art, " I determined not to know anything among you save Jesus Christ and Him crucified?" Nor was it old Roman, and Jew, and Greek, who entertained alone this opposition to the Gospel

—this criminal shame of its central cardinal theme. Alas! human nature, to this hour, remains unchanged, and the offence of the cross will never cease. 'What!' says the pride of intellect, and the pride of reason, and the pride of self-righteousness, 'am I to stand indebted for salvation, to a crucified Man, to a dead God? Is a mangled body and an accursed cross, the oracle from which the Lord Almighty is to address His rational creatures? Am I, moreover, to get heaven, just as a beggar gets his alms—nothing of the purchase-price my own —all from the doing and dying of another?' Yes! it is even so. "The foolishness of God is wiser than men, and the weakness of God is stronger than men." "The preaching of the cross is to them that perish foolishness; but to them that are saved, it is *the power of God*." And though now, Roman pride may scorn it, and Jewish bigotry may frown on it, and Greek philosophy may discard it; yet the day is coming, when Roman, Jew, Greek, Barbarian, Scythian, bond and free, will own that thorn-crowned MAN, as "King of kings and Lord of lords!"

II. We come now to the second clause. This Gospel of Christ is "*the power of God* (or, omitting the article, which is not in the original, "*power of God*,"—God's own instrumental means of saving men),—"*Power of God unto salvation.*" Of the dominant power at present in the world, we have reason to be "ashamed;" —the power of brute force—the monster-power of war—the power associated with Paganism and the savage ages. Let us confront the demon-power with the angel-power—the power which has been earth's greatest curse, with the power which has proved earth's greatest blessing—the power of guilty man to destruction, with the power of Almighty God "unto salvation." Without that Gospel of Christ, the world had not one ray of light on the subject of salvation, either from the guilt or the dominion of sin. Oratory, poetry, philosophy, taste, intellect, reason, were all baffled and confounded; professing themselves on this great mystery to be wise, they became fools. The world had tried for ages and generations to solve the problem; but every oracle was dumb on the great question, "What must I do to be saved?" The Greek might discourse on the loveliness of nature;—he might speak of the theology of mountains and groves and forests and rivers. Yes, truly. We allow they *are* witnesses to the power of God:—we have no wish to depreciate their testimony. St Paul had none. He, surely, was feelingly alive to the glories of nature's scenery, who, standing on that same occasion to which we have already adverted, on Mars Hill, with their Acropolis before him, could, to the Athenians, so sublimely discourse on "God who made the world and all things therein, who dwelleth not in temples" (such temples as these! —pointing up to their adjoining Parthenon), "made with hands;"* or to the Lystrians, as he spake of "the living God, who made heaven, and the earth, and the sea, and all things that are therein; who giveth rain from heaven, and fruitful seasons, filling our hearts with food and with gladness."† But listen, ye Greeks! Pile, if you will, mountain on mountain; ransack all the

---

* Acts xvii. 24. † Acts xiv. 17.

glories of material nature; bring every flower that blooms, and every torrent that sweeps in wild music to the sea; summon old ocean from his deep caverns, and the myriad stars that gem the firmament! They may, and do, silently and eloquently, speak on the theme of God's "eternal power and Godhead." But there is *one* theme on which "they have no speech nor language,— their voice is not heard," and that is, *How is God to deal with my sinful soul?* With regard to this question, you have nothing to draw with, and the well is deep.

Is there, then, no answer elsewhere? Yes; where the volume of nature fails, the volume of Inspiration interposes. The question *is* answered. The Gospel of Christ is "the power of God unto salvation;" or, as St Paul expresses it in a kindred passage, "Christ crucified is the power of God!" He is the Power of God to atone for sin. He is the Power of God to satisfy justice, and meet the requirements of the law. He is the Power of God to rob death of its sting, and the grave of its victory. We hear much of the bygone power of man. The Nile, the

Euphrates, the Tiber, are washing, to this hour, the colossal memorials of that power. His sovereignty, too, in these later days, over the elements, is a mighty thing;—his making the winged lightning his ambassador, annihilating space, converting the world into a vast whispering-gallery;—tidings from these awful battle-fields, or secrets in which the fate of empires and centuries are suspended, transmitted by a magic touch from capital to capital;—the power of steam, too, like a fiery spirit, careering majestically over land and ocean. But what is his power when brought to bear on the soul, and the sinner, and eternity? A voice is heard saying of, and to, all human might:—"Thus far shalt thou go, and no further: here let thy proud waves be stayed." The world, as we have seen, had given it long eras to work out, if it could, the problem of its own self-restoration. But after these centuries of failure; after God had given man his own time and means to exhaust every effort to save himself, He says,— 'Now, listen to My own divine expedient: By lifting up my beloved Son on the cross, I intend to draw all men unto Me!' Verily here is a new *power*,—" a new thing" on the earth. The world is to be conquered; society is to be remoulded; time-honoured religions are to be overthrown; Pantheons are to be subverted; aye, better than all, souls are to be saved, by the Power of a silent transforming principle. " The battle of the warrior is with confused noise, and garments rolled in blood: but this shall be with burning and fuel of fire." " HE shall not strive nor cry, nor cause His voice to be heard in the streets. A bruised reed shall He not break, and the smoking flax shall He not quench: He shall bring forth judgment unto truth." As the silent energies of nature (such as electricity and gravitation) are the mightiest of all,—so is it with this spiritual one. And the marvellous thing is, that it is a silent Power, dealing with hostile, opposing, counteractive elements. It finds the soul in a state of disorganisation; the Power unto salvation has to confront powers unto destruction. It is Light in conflict with Darkness. But it is *the Power of God;* and over this wreck, this moral chaos, He has only to utter the mandate, "Let there be light," and light shall be. Ah! there is no power that can bind the soul, or, rather, that can *un*-bind its fetters, like this! You remember the maniac, of old, who dwelt among the tombs. No *man* could bind him. They had tried it; but he had burst their ligaments like tow, and roamed that dark graveyard. At last he spied on the white strand of Gennesaret, ONE of whom he had heard. It was *Jesus!* See him now, sitting "clothed, and in his right mind." So with the soul still. There are many, who, in the mad fever of their passions, have roamed for years amid the place of the dead, "crying and cutting themselves with stones." But the Divine Redeemer, in the glories of His Person,—in the completeness of His work,—has stood before them. Unbindable, untamable, by all human means, they have taken a child's place at the foot of His cross; and there they now are, sitting, with the peace of Heaven mirrored in their hearts; "the joy of the Lord their strength."

III. Let us advert, finally, to the third clause. "*To every one that believeth.*" After unfolding this great salvation,—the most gracious and glorious expression of God's own "power,"—we are naturally led to ask, who are the favoured recipients? what are their rare qualifications? Is it the godly, the virtuous, the rich, the learned? Nay. It is, "*to every one that believeth.*" "Every one." The water of the wayside pool is not more free, than are the blessings of that Gospel. The poorest barbarian in the mountains of Pisidia,—the ragged outcast among the purlieus of Corinth,—the ignorant savage on the rocks of Malta,—the Tiberias fisherman, or the blind beggar on the Palestine highway,—were not less welcome to the foot of the cross, than the learned Apollos, the Roman Prætor, or the high-born courtier of Nero's household.

Nor is Christ crucified only *free* to all. He is also suited for all. Amid all the diversities of country, climate, language, manners, civilisation; in the polished age, the uncivilised age, the philosophic age, the war age, the utilitarian age,—the human heart is found the same : and the One Physician, the one medicine, " Christ crucified," able to heal *all* diseases. To every one! We may follow the sun in his fiery course as he circles the globe, and in vain shall we search for the spot on which he shines, where this Gospel may not be freely proclaimed. The quality of water is not affected by the nature of the vessel which contains it; the water is the same, whether it be taken in a golden goblet, or an earthen jar;—by the king holding it in his jewelled cup, or the beggar that has no cup but the palm of his hands. So is it with the water in the wells of Salvation. Around these, the rich and poor, naturally and spiritually, meet together; and whether it be with vessels of great, or vessels of small quantity,—vessels of cups or vessels of flagons,—the invitation is the same, " Whosoever will, let him take the water of life freely." " Him that cometh unto Me" (irrespective of all sins, shortcomings, moral disabilities) " I will in no wise cast out." Look at that scene in the early Church, Peter and John healing the impotent man at the Beautiful Gate of the Temple. It was an acted parable of the Gospel-power of God unto salvation. That helpless cripple, at the all-powerful name of "JESUS OF NAZARETH," cast aside his crutches, rose from his couch of abject helplessness, with strength in his powerless limbs, and praise on his long-sealed lips. And next day, when the two apostles were summoned before the high priest, with the rulers, and elders, and scribes, and interrogated thus, "By what *power*, or by what name, have ye done this?" Peter nobly replied (and it is a reply applicable to every diseased, helpless, sin-stricken sinner, who has risen from his couch of misery and entered the Temple of grace, walking, and leaping, and praising God), "If we be this day examined of the good deed done to the impotent man, by what means he is made whole; be it known unto you all, and to all the people of Israel, that by the name of *Jesus Christ of Nazareth*, whom ye crucified, whom God raised from the dead, even by HIM doth this man stand here before you whole" (Acts iv. 9, 10).

Such, then, was the announcement of Paul's purpose in coming to ROME. Such, rather, let us repeat, was the watchword and life-motto of this great soldier of the cross, from the hour he assayed his armour, till the hour, in this city of his closing years, he laid that armour down, and the good fight was finished. We shall find afterwards, how nobly he was able to redeem his pledge and uphold his testimony. With the dungeon-gloom around him, and anticipations more terrible still for flesh and blood before him, yet with the loved name and cause on his lips and in his heart, he could make the dying avowal, "For the which cause I also suffer these things; nevertheless, I am *not ashamed.*"

Brethren, let me ask, in conclusion, the great practical question, Have *you* made this Gospel of Christ the power of God to *your* salvation? Do you cleave with full purpose of heart to its glorious central truth—

"This all my hope—this all my plea—
That Jesus lived and died for me?"

and are you jealous of aught interfering with

it? It is said of one of the great Venetian painters, that, when completing a picture of the marriage in Cana of Galilee, in which the adorable Redeemer was to form the central and prominent figure, he observed some golden cups and goblets introduced in the foreground, which served to divert the eye from the main Personage. He immediately took his brush and erased them from the canvas. The incident has been beautifully used by a well-known Christian writer to describe and illustrate the place which Christ and Him crucified should have in the believer's creed and the believer's heart. Let it stand out by itself in solitary power and grandeur. Let nothing be suffered to detract from it. Let all other accessories be subordinate. Let them serve only to bring into bolder and grander relief, HIM, who is "the chiefest among ten thousand, and altogether lovely." Everything else on which you peril your soul's safety is a refuge of lies—

"On Christ, the solid Rock, I stand;
All other ground is sinking sand."

And, believe me, especially there is one place

—there is one *time*, above all others, when that glorious method of salvation will be found and owned to be the only upholding—the only saving power. Undervalue it as you may while you live, it will not be so in the last solemn moments. Who that has witnessed a death-bed scene, but must have observed how all other trusts and confidences, all other dogmas, and doctrines, and questions, pale into insignificance. There is no name but One, *then*. The tongue can find no room—the heart can find space for nothing else but *this*—" Christ crucified the Power of God." It is not ministers, nor churches, nor rituals, nor creeds, nor rubrics then! It is "the blood," sprinkled in that midnight of awe and mystery on the soul's doorposts, which alone speaks peace, when the destroying angel—the king of Terrors—is passing by. "None but Christ! none but Christ!" was the utterance of the dying Lambert at the stake. They are the same words which have awoke the silent echoes of ten thousand death-chambers, and hung on millions of dying lips.

May the music of that name and the music of that theme gladden us through life! May they cheer our souls in their passage through "the dark Valley of the shadow!"

SERMON II.

Paul's Letter to the Romans; Its Great Theme.

" So, as much as in me is, I am ready to preach the gospel to you that are at Rome also. For I am not ashamed of the gospel of Christ: for it is the power of God unto salvation to every one that believeth; to the Jew first, and also to the Greek. FOR THEREIN IS THE RIGHTEOUSNESS OF GOD REVEALED from faith to faith: as it is written, the just shall live by faith."—ROM. i. 15–17.

" But what things were gain to me, those I counted loss for Christ. Yea doubtless, and I count all things but loss for the excellency of the knowledge of Christ Jesus my Lord: for whom I have suffered the loss of all things, and do count them but dung, that I may win Christ, and be found in Him, not having mine own righteousness, which is of the law, but that which is through the faith of Christ, the righteousness which is of God by faith."—PHIL. III. 7–9.

II.

(*Preached at the Porta del Popolo, February* 26, 1871.)

ROM. i. 17.

"For therein is the righteousness of God revealed."

LAST Lord's day, I entered on a brief series of discourses illustrative of incidents in the life of St Paul, bearing on his connection with this ancient capital of the Roman Empire. I began with the announcement of his own purpose and resolve in coming hither, viz., to preach the Gospel of Christ, as "the power of God unto salvation." To-day, I would venture to direct your thoughts to what may still be deemed a preliminary theme; but it is one which cannot well be passed in silence. Not only does it form the second special proposition consequent on the Apostle's announcement, "I am ready to preach the Gospel to you that are in ROME also. . . . . (*For*, therein is *the righte-*

ousness of God revealed);" but it is the subject, of all others, specially interwoven with his great Epistle to the early Church in this city.

I need not further premise, by reminding you of the place that Epistle itself occupies, alike in the writings of the Apostle, and in the canon of inspired Scripture. It is the sublimest which issued from his pen;—the most logical, argumentative, conclusive,—an epitome and compendium of divine truth. More than this, it is a repertory of comfort. And we may well ask, when or where was an "Afflicted man's companion" more needed or more welcome, than when that letter was sent within the gates of the metropolis? For what was the position the Christians there occupied? Truly, they were as sheep in the midst of wolves. An inhuman tyrant was reigning in the halls of Cæsar; while an obsequious multitude were too ready, with fire and sword, to carry out his behests of cruelty against the hated Nazarenes. They were trembling on the edge of a volcano;—the slumbering forces ready at any moment to burst forth. Poor human nature would, at times, be under strong temptation to abandon the struggle, to surrender the unequal fight, and abjure the name of Christ. It is for these brave yet desponding believers the cheering words of the Epistle were penned. It is the rallying-cry of their great hero,—the trumpet-blast to nerve and prepare them for the battle. Take one extract from it;—that which is contained in the matchless eighth chapter. How their eyes would kindle, and their faltering courage revive, as they read aloud of "no condemnation to them that are in Christ Jesus!"* Called to the renunciation of beloved earthly ties, how would they be braced to the sacrifice and endurance, as they traced the glowing lines, "Who shall separate us from the love of Christ?"† When summoned to more cruel tortures, how the precious words of the divine keepsake would sustain their mangled frames,—"I reckon that the sufferings of this present time are not worthy to be compared with the glory which shall be revealed!"‡ How would it serve to mitigate the

---

* Rom. viii. 1.   † Rom. viii. 35.   ‡ Rom. viii. 18.

I

gloom of the dungeon, or the horrors of the circus, their repeating to one another, "We know that all things work together for good to them that love God?"* As Romans, too, their grandest dream, once at least, was that of conquest: how would they be animated, as they heard of something far transcending the triumphs of those garlanded heroes they had seen, oft and again, passing along their Via Sacra and ascending the steps of their Capitol? As Christ's warriors, how would they be sustained with the thought, that by loyal adhesion to His cause and fidelity to death, they would be made, at last, "more than conquerors"† through Him that loved them.

But it is not to its treasures of comfort and consolation I desire, now, to direct your attention, but rather to the great doctrinal key-note of the Apostle's teaching in that remarkable Letter; what would doubtless, also, form the key-note to his oral ministrations, when his longing wish came to be fulfilled, "to *preach* the Gospel

---

* Rom. viii. 28. † Rom. viii. 37.

to you that are in ROME also." After an irresistible, we may rather say, a humiliating demonstration of our fallen state by nature,—that "by deeds of law no flesh living can be justified,"—bringing in a culprit-world "guilty before God," he proceeds to explain and enforce the topic of which we are now to speak. Having discovered and laid bare the disease, he reveals the antidote and remedy. He reaches the height of his high argument, in the revelation of "THE RIGHTEOUSNESS OF GOD." "For therein is *the Righteousness of God* revealed from faith to faith." "Now the Righteousness of God without the law is manifest, . . . even *the Righteousness of God*, which is by faith of Jesus Christ, unto all and upon all them that believe." "We are made *the Righteousness of God* in Him." "That as sin hath reigned unto death, even so might grace reign through *righteousness* unto eternal life, by Jesus Christ our Lord."* It is the Word—the Theme—we shall come to find on his tongue when the last

---

* Rom. i. 17; iii. 21, 22; v. 21.

shadows are falling : the music of the same keynote of his Roman letter, lingers in sustained energy in his dying song, and forms the closing glorious outburst of his dying lips,—" Henceforth there is laid up for me a crown of *righteousness*, which the Lord, the righteous Judge, will give me at that day."

We shall state the general doctrine, as that is unfolded in other parts of Scripture, as well as in this Epistle ; and then speak of its experimental power and bearing, on the history and teaching of the great Apostle.

The Believer needs a positive as well as a negative justification. It is not enough, that, on account of the vicarious sufferings and death of his great Redeemer, he stand acquitted at the bar of God, with the sentence (so to speak) of "not guilty" pronounced upon him. " The righteous Lord loveth *righteousness*." At the entrance-gate of heaven the summons is heard, " Open ye the gates, that the *righteous* nation, which keepeth the truth, may enter in." It is "*the righteous*" who shall go into "life eternal." "Then shall *the righteous* shine forth as the sun in the glory of the Father." Paradise lost, involved the loss of righteousness; Paradise regained, is the regaining of the forfeited blessing. But if the King's daughter must be thus "all glorious," her "clothing of wrought gold," where is the shuttle to fabricate the gorgeous tissue? In other words, where is such Righteousness, in the unqualified sense of the term, denoting absolute moral perfection, to be found? Where is this perfect coincidence of the human will with the divine? Can man himself effect or secure it? "There is none," and there *can* be none, thus "righteous, no not one." The holiest and the best, weighed in the balances, are found wanting. God's strongest cedars have quivered and bent and fallen under the blast of temptation. God's best heroes and saintliest men have been "of like passions" after all. They have nobly fought, indeed; but have again and again succumbed in the battles of the soul—mournful impotence and failure side by side with gigantic deeds. They enter heaven covered with the scars of the enemy; with ruffled plumes in the helmet of salvation. To stand on the great Day of judgment attired in this their own imperfect righteousness! The fire of God would burn up its gossamer threads, and leave them naked and speechless. Hear the testimony and averment, in this very Epistle, of the boldest and the best of these heavenly warriors, as to the shortcomings and deficiency of his loftiest aims and efforts: "The good that I would, I do not; but the evil which I would not, that I do."* Or of an older saint still, "Though I wash myself with snow-water and make my hands never so clean, yet wilt Thou plunge me in the ditch, and mine own clothes shall abhor me." † If the sinner, then, despair of having a *personal*, he must have a *borrowed* righteousness; he must stand indebted to another, for what he cannot obtain for himself. Like the Hebrews of old at the Exodus, he must not only go forth from Egypt with his chains broken, but with borrowed jewels. With " earrings of gold, and chains and

---

* Rom. vii. 19.   † Job ix. 30.

bracelets of silver," he must march onwards to the promised land; and that spangled attire, in which God's spiritual Israel are robed, is the glorious Righteousness which Christ wrought out by the obedience of His life.

Brethren, let us have clear and distinct ideas of what that Righteousness is. Let us not blur the peerless truth. Let us not pare. it down or defraud it of its own grand symmetry and proportions. Let us not think of it as merely implying that Christ has set before us an absolute example of human excellence,—a perfect divine copy,—which we are to seek to imitate. Were it so, from being a doctrine of surpassing comfort, it would rather lead to a depressing and hopeless despondency. Gazing on that spotless Model, would only more assuredly convince of the utter impossibility of ever attaining to any measure of acceptable obedience. It would only bring home to the soul, a crushing, overwhelming sense of its own deficiencies, and fill it with dismay at the thought of standing at the tribunal of a holy God! But that Righteousness is *imputed*—put down to our account—

reckoned as if it were our own. We stand accepted, in the garment of our Elder Brother. Listen to some Scripture testimonies on this great truth. "I bring near," says God, "My Righteousness."* Daniel speaks of the advent of Messiah the Prince, after seventy weeks of years, "to finish transgression, and to make an end of sins, and to make reconciliation for iniquity, and to bring in everlasting righteousness." † "I will greatly rejoice in the Lord," says the believer, or the Church, in the prophecies of Isaiah; "my soul shall be joyful in my God; for He hath clothed me with the garments of salvation, He hath covered me with a robe of righteousness."‡ "This is the name whereby He shall be called, the Lord our Righteousness."§ Not to enumerate other references in this Epistle to the same theme, in the fifth chapter, the Apostle draws a beautiful parallelism between the two Adams—the one, "of the earth, earthy;" the other, "the Lord from heaven:" the two federal heads or representa-

---

* Isa. xlvi. 15. † Dan. ix. 24.
‡ Isa. lxi. 10. § Jer. xxiii. 6

tives of the two covenants,—the covenant of works, and the covenant of grace. In the one case, the sin of the first Adam has been imputed to all his posterity. We have fallen in him; the taint of corruption and the penalty of death has been transmitted by him from generation to generation. I do not pause to examine the difficulties of that doctrine. However strange and anomalous it may seem that we should be made to stand responsible for the guilt and doings of another;—however pride and reason may reject and repudiate the truth,—I take it as it stands, a recorded fact, a solemn statement in the Word of God. But if there be apparent mystery in the doctrine of the imputation of sin, objection to that doctrine, if not disarmed, is surely at least neutralised, by looking at it, side by side, with the glorious parallel and counterpart truth—that the Righteousness of Jehovah-Jesus, the federal Head of the second covenant, is in the same manner imputed to all who believe. "As by the offence of one, judgment came upon all men unto condemnation; even so by the righteousness of one, the free gift came upon all men unto justification of life. For as by one man's disobedience many were made sinners, so by the obedience of one shall many be made righteous."*

Such, then, is the truth contained in the text; —Jesus, the Lamb of God, in His life of sinless obedience, has procured that robe for me. He has not only *died* in my room, to save me from sin's penalty, but He has *lived* in my room, to present me with a free gift of spotless righteousness. All that wondrous life of His, from the cradle to the cross, was a weaving of the needed garment; His kindness, His love, His unselfishness, His submission, His humility, His meek acquiescence in His Father's will, all these have been put down to my account, reckoned as if. I had done them. By casting this divinely-wrought garment over us, all our blemishes and shortcomings and deficiencies are covered and concealed. The eye of a holy God, in looking upon us, can see "neither spot nor

---

* Rom. v. 18, 19.

wrinkle, nor any such thing." "See," exclaims the Psalmist, as he screens himself behind the burnished shield of this glorious Righteousness, hiding all his own defects and unworthiness, —" See God our shield, look on the face of Thine Anointed!"

Shall we go to the outer world for some image to illustrate this great doctrine? You have seen, in our own land, summer's dying sun bathing the hills in a blaze of light. The dark purple summits, the rugged corries, the splintered granite peaks, were all hid from view, buried and lost in the excess of that setting radiance. That is the picture of the soul, with all its yawning chasms of guilt and vileness, lost and hidden in the glory of Christ's righteousness. You have seen the rugged root of some unsightly tree cast into a fire. Its ruggedness is lost in the flames; it has itself soon become one mass of ruby splendour. So with the soul cast into this glowing fire of "imputed righteousness"—the eye even of Infinite purity can see nothing but a mass of radiant glory. Or, shall we go again for typical illustration, to the surer page of Scripture? Open the Old Testament, teeming as it is with pictures of the great coming salvation, and behold both phases of the work of Jesus, atoning for sin by His death, and working out righteousness by His life: God hath joined them together, and let not man put them asunder! We love to look at the impressive type of the scapegoat,—the hands of the priest laid upon its head, and the innocent animal bearing the imputed load away to a land of oblivion. We see, in this, the representation of the former truth—our sins laid on the head of the surety Saviour. But I go to other symbols. I go to the earliest type of all, and see the glorious doctrine of Christ's imputed righteousness shining amid the blighted bowers of Eden. I see the guilty pair at first screening their nakedness with the covering of fig leaves sewed together, but which are speedily superseded by other garments divinely gifted and provided (Gen. iii. 7–21). These "coats of skins," we have every reason to believe, were those of animals slain in sacrifice: if so, they formed, surely, expressive emblems of the garment of righteousness provided through the obedience and death of a mightier Victim, the Lamb thus "slain from the foundation of the world." Or shall we take a later typical vision. Joshua, the High priest, the type and representative of the ransomed sinner, stands before the Lord. He is a redeemed man,—his sins are forgiven,—he is a "brand plucked from the burning." But see his dress: he is attired in filthy garments. High priest as he was—redeemed as he was—a monument of grace—he stands in tattered clothing. What says the covenant angel? He strips off the miserable vestments, clothes him with change of raiment, and sets "a fair mitre on his head." Behold the living picture of Christ's righteousness put upon us! From being clad in beggars' garments, "wretched, and miserable, and poor, and blind, and naked," we are royally robed, royally crowned. We are made "kings and priests unto God," and arrayed as such. What says the believer in the song? "I am black but comely:" black in my own righteousness, comely through the righteousness and comeliness of another. How could the Lord address His Church in that same precious portion of Scripture, unless He regarded it as a fortress gleaming with a glory not its own? "Thy neck is like the tower of David, builded for an armoury, whereon there hang a thousand bucklers, all shields of mighty men." Nor need we pause with the recorded testimony of the Church in ancient times. What formed the theme of the glorious company of Apostles and the goodly fellowship of prophets, has been the precious jewel in the creed of holy men of all subsequent ages. See how Luther clings to it:—"He gives me what is His, and I give Him what is mine; I give Him all my sins, and He gives me back in exchange, all His righteousness."

And although on this we cannot now enter, full and ample is the warrant for receiving and appropriating the offered garment. "The righteousness of God which is by faith of Jesus Christ, is unto all, and upon *all them that believe*, for there is no difference." * The

---
* Rom. iii. 22.

Elder Brother has a treasury filled with these garments—"the best robe" of the parable. All that we need is to use the key of faith to unlock it:—"It is the righteousness which is of God *by faith*." Accept it; reach forth the hand of faith to take this richer robe than Tyrian loom ever wrought—this garment of richer gold than Ophir mines ever produced. It is not beyond the reach of one here present. Listen to God's own inspired description of it in this same Epistle:—"The righteousness which is of faith speaketh on this wise, Say not in thine heart who shall ascend into Heaven?" (*i.e.*, it does not ask you to attempt the impossibility of scaling the heavens to bring it down), "or who shall descend into the deep?" (it does not demand a similar impossibility of descending into the depths of the sea or the caverns of the earth to bring it up). "But what saith it? The word is nigh thee, even in thy mouth and in thy heart, the word of faith which we preach" (Rom. x. 6-8).

Touching and very instructive is this subject

in connection with the life and character of that great Apostle whose footsteps we are now tracking in this city of his habitation. In a letter of his (a portion of which we read at this morning's service), written not *to* Rome, but *from* Rome, to his best-loved Church at Philippi, his first-begotten children in the Gentile world, we find him enumerating particularly his "gains,"—his rare catalogue of natural virtues and religious privileges; what the world would have called 'a splendid righteousness.' How many would have coveted him,—lived and died, happy, in the conscious possession of so distinguished a stock of merit! "If any other man thinketh that he hath whereof he might trust in the flesh, I more: circumcised the eighth day, of the stock of Israel, of the tribe of Benjamin, an Hebrew of the Hebrews; as touching the law, a Pharisee; . . . touching the righteousness which is in the law, blameless. But," he adds, "what things were gain to me, those I counted loss for Christ."* And it must indeed have been no

---

* Phil. iii. 4-7.

small effort for him, to discard all he once so fondly loved and prized, and to which he so proudly clung. Sad to go to that gallery of pleasant pictures which he himself had hung in the chambers of his soul, and with his own hand to wrench one by one from its place;—to tear sculpture by sculpture from niche and pedestal, and to write upon these walls, so lately gleaming with fancied righteousness, "*All loss for Christ.*" The seaman does not grudge taking to pieces his old rotten boat; demolishing some miserable craft, with gaping sides and worm-eaten timbers. It costs him not a thought to have it broken up and destroyed. But that noble ship of Tarshish, just launched from the docks, in the pride of conscious inherent strength, and filled with precious stores! it could not be, without an effort, that the owner (convinced of some irremediable defect), brings it back to port, takes it asunder, timber by timber, stripping it of its garniture and beauty. So it was with St Paul. He saw that the vessel of legal and ceremonial righteousness, with all its pride of form and bearing, could not weather

K

the storm. These frescoed pictures on the walls of his heart, are, in the eye of God and of His holy law, only daubs of untempered mortar. *He* was led to see, what others might not—that on the Great Day, all that once boasted righteousness would be but as "wood and hay and stubble." It would avail him nothing as a ground of justification :—a poor miserable counterfeit : "The day of the Lord of Hosts shall be upon all the ships of Tarshish, and upon all pleasant pictures!" And he adds, "Yea doubtless, and I count all but loss for the excellency of the knowledge of Christ Jesus my Lord : for whom I have suffered the loss of all things."[*]

In these words, he has undoubtedly reference to that wild night in the sea of Adria, when pursuing his voyage to Rome in the Alexandrian corn-ship. The tempest was threatening; the safety of the ship seemed to demand a lightening of the cargo. But that precious corn! must it be sacrificed for the safety of the vessel? It was "gain;" but must it come to be reckoned

---

[*] Phil. iii. 8.

as "loss," and tossed overboard? Yes, the tempest decides the question. It must be consigned to the waves, otherwise the vessel will founder. There is no room for debate; the crew make up their minds to "suffer the loss of all." Nay more, when the tempest howls with greater fury, and danger and death stare them full in the face, they go a step further. The "loss" is never thought of. They do not now pause in uncertainty and indecision, saying, 'Cannot we spare these precious barrels of merchandise?' Imminent danger makes them glad to plunge them into the roaring sea. When the question is between the loss of the wheat, and the loss of the ship, there can be no hesitation. They account them as absolutely worthless—of no value. They are glad to see them pitching against one another in the dark abyss. They look upon them now, not as gain or treasure, but as having proved an absolute hindrance, endangering their safety.

And this was the process in St Paul's mind. First, there was a clinging to all these birth-right gains, and self-righteous confidences. He was loath to part with them. Secondly, he underwent the "loss," but it was accompanied with "suffering." It was a violent effort to him to renounce all which he had once so fondly treasured and trusted in. But the third stage of feeling was when he was brought to say, 'I *hate* them all: they are as dung: they are worthless: they are imperilling the vessel's safety; they are endangering my soul's interest; let them go every one of them! They were once "gain to me;" once I endured "suffering" at the thought of losing them; but now, heave them all into the raging sea. I have learnt to hate them. I count them as refuse, sweepings, husks, "that I may win Christ, and be found in him."'

Is this our case? Can we, as voyagers on the sea of life, make such a protestation, that all in which we once trusted and gloried, as a ground of justification in the sight of God,—our good name, our good doings, our moralities, and natural virtues and amiabilities and alms-deeds, our acts of kindness and sterling integrity and unselfish benevolence,—these we toss overboard, in order that the giant deed of Christ's doing and dying may stand out alone in solitary grandeur? "Not having mine own righteousness, which is of the law, but that which is through the faith of Christ, the righteousness which is of God by faith." Oh! there is no other garment for the soul to cover its spiritual nakedness;—there is no other rest for the soul burdened with the sense of its shortcomings. Not only is it the dove hidden in the clefts of the smitten Rock (*that* is the image of pardon and safety); but it is the dove, too, soaring aloft to the celestial windows in the borrowed plumage of a glorious righteousness;—its wings "covered with silver, and its feathers with yellow gold." It is a truth which may well bring with it peace and joy and elevation of heart. "The effect of righteousness is quietness and assurance for ever." "We which believe do enter into rest," 'and that,' quaintly says an old writer, 'by ceasing from our own works, as God, on the seventh day, did from His.'

If it be a blessed truth to live on, what a

blessed truth to die on! What a joyous garment this, wherewith to wrap us round when the billows are high, and we are plunging into Jordan! We can imagine, when that solemn hour arrives; when, perhaps suddenly, we are laid on the pillow from which we are to rise no more; and when, despite of our well-grounded confidence in the Gospel, gloomy visions and memories of former guilt *will* gather around, filling us with trembling and dismay,—oh! in the midst of the thick darkness, to feel girded with a panoply, which the rush of waters cannot penetrate, and of which the King of terrors cannot despoil us—the robe which we got at the cross, and which we are to wear before the throne!

Yes, children of God, of every age and rank and experience, tune your hearts and lips for the joyous strain! Aged believers, sing it! ye whose earthly, pilgrim-garments are soiled and travel-worn, but whose robe of righteousness is fresh as in the day of your espousals with the Heavenly Bridegroom. Young believers, sing it! ye who may have but recently stood at the marriage-altar with your Lord, and received at His hands the glistering vesture; who may have a long journey, it may be, still to traverse, ere you reach the King's Palace. Sorrowing believers, sing it! take down your harps from the willows of sadness. Ye are in mourning attire; but through your weeds there shines this bright clothing of wrought gold, which the shadows of death and the grave cannot dim or alloy. Dying ones, sing it! if our voice could reach you from this place, whether ye be old or young, rich or poor; the aged pilgrim of heaven, falling gently, like a shock of corn in its season, or the child, whose lips early grace has perfected with praise—going to an early crown: Oh! let the whole Church of the living God, divided on other themes,—dumb and mute with other songs,—join together in glad acclaim, kindle into holy rapture with this—

> "Jesus, Thy blood and righteousness
> My beauty are, my glorious dress;
> 'Mid flaming worlds, in these array'd,
> With joy I shall lift up my head.

"This spotless robe the same appears
When ruin'd nature sinks in years;
No age can change its glorious hue—
The robe of Christ is ever new.

"And when the dead shall hear Thy voice,
And all Thy banish'd ones rejoice,
Their beauty this, their glorious dress,—
JESUS THE LORD OUR RIGHTEOUSNESS!"

SERMON III.

St Paul's Fellowships in Rome: Timothy.

"To all that be in Rome, beloved of God, called to be saints: Grace to you, and peace, from God our Father, and the Lord Jesus Christ."—ROM. i. 7.

"To TIMOTHY, MY DEARLY BELOVED SON: Grace, mercy, and peace, from God the Father, and Christ Jesus our Lord. I thank God, whom I serve from my forefathers with pure conscience, that without ceasing I have remembrance of thee in my prayers night and day; greatly desiring to see thee, being mindful of thy tears, that I may be filled with joy; when I call to remembrance the unfeigned faith that is in thee, which dwelt first in thy grandmother Lois, and thy mother Eunice; and I am persuaded that in thee also."—2 TIM. i. 2-5

III.

(Preached at the Porta del Popolo, March 5, 1871.)

2 TIM. i. 2.

"Timothy, my dearly beloved son."

IN prosecuting our theme of St Paul's residence at ROME, there can be no subject of deeper interest to us than his fellowships with Roman Christians. It is evident from the perusal of the closing chapter in his Epistle, that before he set foot personally in this city, there was already within its walls the nucleus of a flourishing Church. In that postscript chapter (if I may so call it), there are twenty-six believers he individually names, to whom he conveys his apostolic salutations, in addition to two of their "households," as well as other "brethren" and "saints" (ver. 14, 15). Several of these were natives of the capital, who, on account of an edict of Claudius, had been expelled from their homes on the Tiber, and driven as fugitives to cities bordering on the Mediterranean. In the places of their exile they had become converts to the faith through the Apostle's preaching. There were others now in Rome, "fervent in spirit, serving the Lord," whom St Paul had not as yet seen in the flesh. They were only known to him by their steadfast faith, devoted lives, and by their "obedience," which, as he expresses it, "had come abroad unto all men" (ver. 19). It is interesting, surely, to know from his own lips, that in his manifold journeyings by land and by sea, whether in his hours of solitude, or where surrounded by busy crowds, ROME and its Church had a constant place in his holiest remembrances; for he specially tells us, that "without ceasing he made mention of them always in his prayers" (Rom. i. 9). We cannot think of him, therefore, coming to this ancient metropolis as to a city of strangers, where he would be isolated from Christian sympathy. In that list of names to which I have just referred, there were doubtless not a few of those "brethren," who, shortly after the Apostle-prisoner landed from his long voyage, met him at Appii Forum; and on seeing whom, after weeks of loneliness and depression, during which no congenial heart had shared the burden of his spirit, he "thanked God and took courage." It is impossible to affirm, whether any reliance can be placed on the identity of the two localities which I visited this last week, credited by tradition as being the dwellings of the Apostle.* Somewhere, at least, we know (and, at all events, it could not probably be far from one or other of these), the members of the infant Church in Rome met him. In "his own hired house," wherever it was (to take up the tone of cheerfulness which characterises the closing words of the Acts), "he received all that came in unto him, preaching the kingdom of God, and teaching those things which concern the Lord Jesus Christ, with all confidence, no man forbidding him."

Among other sacred fellowships, however,

---

* See the description of this visit in Introductory Chapter, p. 29, *et seq*.

there is one which stands out with special and pre-eminent distinctiveness. While all who were begotten in the Lord were dear to the Apostle, TIMOTHY has a peculiar halo of interest encircling him, not more in connection with previous years, than with St Paul's Roman residence. For no one does he long more fervently to come to his house or to his dungeon. When the last days—the last hours, had arrived, how vehemently does he desire his presence! In his second letter, how touching to read twice over, as if to make doubly sure, "Do thy diligence to come shortly to me." "Do thy diligence," he repeats, "to come before winter." We are not told, but we can, at all events, entertain the possibility (the probability), that these appeals were not in vain. We love to dwell on the likelihood of the last closing moments being soothed by the presence and voice most prized by him; Timothy walking by his side on the Ostian Road, supporting and cheering the Christian hero in his great trial-hour, with those hopes full of immortality, which he himself had so oft proclaimed to others. Though it may be no more than a gratuitous fiction, we felt it, at all events, alike pleasing and impressive, two days ago, in the magnificent Basilica of the San Paolo, to gaze on the juxtaposition of their tombs; the ashes of the great Apostle and of his beloved companion resting traditionally side by side. "They were lovely and pleasant in their lives, and in their death they were not divided." One could not help feeling, that often as the epitaph had been used, it was never more fitting and appropriate than here.*

In adverting for a little to the history of Timothy, let us glance, in their order, at his *Youth*, his *Conversion*, and his *Work*.

In speaking of the *earlier* passages of his life, we must change for a moment the scene from ROME, the hired house, the dungeon, and the place of martyrdom, to a distant city in Asia Minor.

---

* See Frontispiece; also Introduction, p. 90.

The family group at Lystra, in Lycaonia, is a pleasing one. The main place, indeed, in that home is vacant. From there being no reference to his father, either in St Paul's letters to Timothy or in the Acts, we are led to conclude that he had died while his boy was yet young. His father, we are expressly told, was not of Hebrew origin, but a Gentile; a Greek by birth and by religion. We also infer that he was a 'proselyte of the gate;' one of those who, in common with the proselytes of righteousness, had abandoned and renounced the errors and debasements of idolatry, and embraced the worship of the God of Israel. Two other members, however, occupy the house, thus probably bereft of its head; the widowed Jewess, the child's mother (by name Eunice), along with her own surviving parent, whom she had evidently taken to her lonely home to be "the nourisher of her old age."

Grace is not hereditary; but it seems to have been so in the case of that mother and daughter in Israel, for the Apostle tells us that they had that richest of dowries, "unfeigned faith." What had brought them to their remote dwelling at Lystra we are not informed. Doubtless, He, who at that same time sent Lydia from her native town, Thyatira, to distant Philippi, had purposes of similar divine grace and mercy in arranging the residence of that Jewish family in this distant city of idolaters. God had blessed their solitude with one object of tender and hallowed interest—"the only son of his mother." The youthful Timothy is beautifully pictured to us, as imbibing his earliest lessons of heavenly wisdom at the feet of these two devout women.

As I have just observed, there is but one characteristic given of the early school in which he was trained. Its lessons were those of "unfeigned faith;" two words, briefly uttered, but fraught with vast significance. From them we infer, that his instructors made him the recipient of their religious belief. He was trained up in the creed of their and his ancestry: from a child he had been taught to "know the Holy Scriptures." Doubtless such faithful guardians would act up rigidly to the solemn charge enjoined in the olden time: " These words which

L

I command thee this day shall be in thine heart, and thou shalt teach them diligently unto thy children, and shalt talk of them when thou sittest in thine house, and when thou walkest by the way, and when thou liest down, and when thou risest up." If other families in that pagan town shared their belief, they may together (as has been pictured), like Lydia and her little band of followers, have resorted Sabbath after Sabbath to the "proseuchæ" or "oratories" by the river-side, and there poured out their hearts in supplication for the blessing of Abraham's God; that He would hasten the coming of the Messiah promised to the Fathers, in whom first Israel, and, through Israel, all the families of the earth were to be blessed. If so, doubtless the child of their many prayers would accompany them to these sacred resorts, and have his mind filled with the hopes of his race,—hopes which had already received their most glorious fulfilment in the advent of the great "Consolation of Israel."

But his was more than mere acquaintance with a theological creed—instruction in the articles of the Hebrew religion. He was taught thus early to admire and love, not only the faith, but the "faith UNFEIGNED," which dwelt in his grandmother Lois and in his mother Eunice. "*Unfeigned faith.*" It was that divine thing, a hallowed, consistent example, the utterances and expressions of a piety that went not forth of "*feigned lips.*" It is too possible now, as it was then, to give an intellectual assent to a round of systematic doctrine,—to be the votaries and disciples of a faith that is *feigned*,—a faith which exercises no ameliorating influence on the heart, no animating and controlling power on the life: a stale, rigid, cold, barren orthodoxy, not countersigned by a corresponding walk and conversation. Not so, was it, in the case of this holy household at Lystra. The injunction of the wise man seems there to have been faithfully followed and fulfilled. "Train" (a word including alike precept and example),—"Train up a child in the way he should go." There was, in these two conscientious Jewish matrons, the true ring of the religious life; not the base counterfeit coin of earth, but the unmistakable currency of heaven.

It was under this hallowed roof, then, that the infancy and childhood and youth of Timothy were spent. But for Lois and Eunice, his would have been an unknown name. The Church of Christ may well go to Lystra, and hang garlands of gratitude around the tomb of these two women in Israel. Blessed the child that is under such a household! Blessed still the children enjoying a mother's prayers! Blessed every one of us, who have the vision of such and similar holy examples, rising up like a green oasis amid the waste of memory!

Let us now turn to his *Call* or *conversion*. This latter word is perhaps out of place and misapplied when used in regard to Timothy. In the history of not a few other characters in holy writ, we can point to some memorable crisis, when, by the power of God's grace and Spirit, a sudden and almost instantaneous change took place in their whole moral natures; when the defiant bulwarks of sin and unbelief and rebellion in a moment fell to the ground, and their entire treasures were surrendered to the Lord,

Such, I need not say, was St Paul himself; when, almost in the twinkling of an eye, the vulture nature was transmuted into that of the dove, that of the lion into the lamb;—when the persecutor, "breathing out threatenings and slaughter," became the child-like follower of Jesus. And many are there still, who can point to similar experiences. 'There, and then, God met me in the way. There was the Jabbok where His angel wrestled with me, and where, in His might I prevailed, and got my new name. There a light, like that on the Damascus highway, brought me to the dust an enemy, a blasphemer, and raised me up a meek disciple. There, in an agony of despair, like the dying felon, I looked on the crucified One, and the gates of mercy were opened to receive me.'

But this is not God's *general* way of procedure. As in nature, there is a process of gradual development towards maturity, "first the blade, then the ear, after that, the full corn in the ear;" as in the animal economy, there is the same gradual progress from infancy and youth to manhood and age; so is it in the spiritual life ; and so was it in the case of Timothy. He could revert to no such momentous turning-point in his history, when his whole being underwent a sudden transformation. His piety had distilled like the dew of heaven, known only by being seen. As we are told that the Jewish temple of old was reared without "hammer, or axe, or tool of iron" being heard; so had the young altar of his faith risen in silence. The soil of his heart had been prepared by godly parental training; the seed sown had been gradually fostered and matured by holy hands.

At the same time, while he thus grew up the child of prayer and of unfeigned faith, an occurrence took place in the city of his dwelling which gave a new impulse to his spiritual life, and altered his whole future destinies. That noble Missionary of heroic faith, with whom he was subsequently to be tenderly associated in this capital, was passing through Lystra, proclaiming the glorious truths of the Gospel. The debased mob, instigated by some opposing Jews who had come from Antioch and Iconium on the evil errand of thwarting his mission, assaulted

St Paul in the open streets with stones, and dragging him outside the city walls, left him there mangled and bleeding. He had apparently anticipated, in thought, his Roman martyrdom, and already joined the "noble army" of these early ages. That life of priceless value was, however, mercifully spared; the furious and cruel attempt only recoiled on the heads of the instigators. It was not without its momentous results. We have every reason to believe that one of the spectators of that outrage was the son of this pious Hebrew home. Accustomed there to the "unfeigned faith" as manifested in the passive virtues of love, and meekness, and submission,—he saw that same "unfeigned faith" manifested in its active form and type of heroic endurance—superiority to physical suffering. The youth's impressible mind, at that impressible period of life, must have been arrested, by (what never fails to arrest and impress)—the conduct of a man in earnest;—one ready to risk his all, and dear life itself, for the sake of the truth. St Paul was bearing about in his cut and lacerated frame "the dying of the Lord Jesus," and in conjunction with this, "the life also of Jesus" (in his meek, calm, and prayerful bearing towards his murderers) was made manifest in his mortal body. In one of its innumerable subsequent instances, the blood of the martyr became the seed of the Church. Next day, he and Barnabas departed from Lystra to Derbe. But they had left ineffaceable footprints behind them. The scene I have just described had stirred the impulses of that young soul. From that hour he claimed a new *home*, a new *father*, a new *name:* "Timothy, my own son in the faith." St Paul returned from his toilsome missionary circuit after an absence of one or two years, to the old scene of his insult and imminent danger. He found a living stone, which had been polishing during his absence, ready now to take its place in the Spiritual Temple; and he could write, as he did on another occasion, in his eventful diary, "The things which happened unto me, have fallen out rather unto the furtherance of the Gospel." The seed sown by pious parents, watered by his own blood and tears, was now, in ripe fruit, gathered by the sickle; this, in its turn, would yield fresh seed to be scattered elsewhere, and give birth to vaster harvests.

God still takes various means of quickening life in His own children,—those who, like Timothy, may have been piously trained, their affections early won to His service. A startling providence—a family bereavement—a time of critical illness—a rousing sermon; these, and such like instrumental agencies, He employs, to give them more living, realising views of the truth, and to stimulate and foster the energies of their spiritual being. They may before have been slumbering, like Elijah, under their juniper-tree; but some Angel has roused them with his quickening touch, and by the bestowal of fresh pledges of divine love and blessing, they go fearlessly on their wilderness way, with an heroic faith to which they were before strangers. Or, like Timothy, they may have received some new and noble impulses from the holy example of others. I believe many of us can similarly revert, in the annals of the past, to some aged friend, or neighbour, or relative, who has perhaps now gone the way of all the earth, but whose beautiful life (the embodiment of all the Christian virtues), has to us invested religion with a charm that *has* never, and *can* never be forgotten. Mere sermons are transient in their impressions,—they may die away with the voice of the speaker. But those life-sermons are imperishable. Timothy *might* forget some passages and sentences in the two Epistles *written* to him by St Paul; but he would never forget that better Epistle, not written with ink; nothing could obliterate its deathless pages. He would never forget that scene of half-completed martyrdom, outside the walls of Lystra; or that other, in long after years (I have already spoken of, as probably witnessed also outside the gates of Rome), when the same devoted champion lay silent under the flash of the sword, which added the greatest to the great cloud of witnesses. Oh for faith and grace, not by word, but by deed, to bear witness to the power and reality of the truth: so that men may take knowledge of us that we have been with Jesus; and when our race is run on earth, though dead we may yet speak!

I pass now briefly to Timothy's *work* and *Apostleship*.

St Paul allowed seven years to elapse before his next return to Lystra. By this time Timothy had outgrown boyhood and youth. He was now ready, as a good soldier, for his armour; prepared to be girded with the panoply of which his spiritual father speaks, when he enjoins him to "war a good warfare." He was not unaware of the perils of such work—the penalties of such a service. For his faithful Instructor had, some years previously, specially reminded him, in common with all the other disciples of these Asiatic cities, that "through much tribulation they must enter into the kingdom of God." But he, as well as the two godly hearts which doated upon him, had counted the cost, and willingly made the sacrifice. They mutually 'remembered the word of the Lord Jesus, how He said, "If any man will come after me, let him deny himself, and take up his cross, and follow me:"—" Whosoever loveth father or mother more than me, is not worthy of me." Both filial and maternal love surrendered to these mightier claims; knowing that whatever forfeiture might be involved in "the present life," in the "world to come," the severed family links would be again renewed in "life everlasting." It is from this time forward that he becomes St Paul's most duteous attendant, and most beloved friend. Lystra, a town of heathen Lycaonia, has the honour of giving a faithful Evangelist to the early Church. As God called Elijah, not from amid the consecrated tribes or cities of Israel, but among the half-Gentile fastnesses of rugged Gilead; so He now finds one of the pillars of His cause, and the main companion of His greatest Apostle, not in Jerusalem or Samaria,—not in Cæsarea or even Antioch, —but in this distant Pagan city. St Paul at once cleaves to him with parental love. The soul of the elder Apostle is knit (like that of David to Jonathan):—" Him would Paul have to go forth with him" (Acts xvi. 3). It is even an illustration of what one sometimes sees, a sympathetic tie binding together those who are naturally of diverse and opposite characters. The fiery Elijah was different from the calm, tranquil Elisha; yet how affectionate and strong was their union! How vehement was Peter's attachment to John, as evidenced by their ever-recurring companionship; and yet how different their temperaments! In the one, the prevailing element was contemplation, gentleness, and love; in the other, heroic and often unregulated impulse and passionate zeal. We see the same here. St Paul had, indeed, a beauteously balanced mind, a fine combination of all spiritual virtues; but the predominating ones were doubtless the masculine—bold, vehement, daring, uncompromising—only once in tears, and that not for himself, or evoked by his own sufferings. Timothy again, as we may gather from St Paul's exhortations to him in the Epistles, inherited more, as it has been called, "the feminine" type of character—wanting in some of the sterner attributes needed for an Apostolic age (1 Cor. xvi. 10); gentle, pliable, sensitive; dissolved in a woman's tenderness when bidding his spiritual Father farewell (2 Tim. i. 4). Even in physical make and constitution he was a contrast to the hardy, wiry man, who could buffet wintry seas and brave summer suns—pass undeterred through countries infested by bandits, and at last endure a winter's dungeon without a cloak to protect him from the cold. Timothy had to be warned against incurring the risk of needless privations. There is a touch of tender interest in the advice of his kind protector (so careless about his own comforts), to take at times "a little wine," to strengthen his unrobust and fragile frame (1 Tim. v. 23). In their after years, too, how great the discrepancy; although in this respect, also, we are not without scriptural antecedents of age clinging lovingly to youth, winter clasping early spring or midsummer in its bosom. It is a New Testament repetition of that beautiful picture of the old economy;—aged Eli, the Priest of the Tabernacle, clinging

with a brother's fondness and confidingness to
the little child who served before the Lord.
Barnabas was St Paul's fellow-labourer; and,
despite of one unhappy occasion of temporary
estrangement, they were no ordinary ties of
affection which linked together these two noble
standard-bearers in the army of the faithful;
but hear, in the Great Apostle's own words,
how tenderer far is his relation to Timothy.
Almost with a father's pride over a much
loved son, he says, "Ye know the proof of him,
that as a *son with the father* he hath served
with me in the Gospel." That filial service,
too, embraced little, trivial things;—things
even referring to his own personal comfort,
which he might have had scruple in devolving
upon others, but which he felt it was using no
liberty to put upon Timothy. Take, for example, that notable glimpse of this easy fami-
liarity and intimacy given us at the close of
the Epistle, and to which I have already incidentally alluded, when he tells him to open
the box at Troas which held his papers and
parchments (probably his private memoranda

and journals, including, it may be, the diploma of Roman citizenship), and bring them along with him to his dungeon; or to fetch the winter cloak (the Roman Pœnula), which had formerly been his companion amid the cutting winds of the Pisidian Mountains, or amid the storms of the Mediterranean. Imagining it would no longer be required, he had inadvertently left it behind him at Troas; but he felt his aged frame needed it now, more than ever, to protect from the pestilential damps of a prison home. "Son Timothy," "My beloved Son," "My own Son in the faith," "My work-fellow," "My brother," are the expressions which bespeak the depth of his affection. Hear how he writes of him when he is looking back on the manifold friendships of a whole life: "I have *no man* like minded." From city to city— and (when separated) from day to day, and from hour to hour—the glory of manhood and the beauty of youth thus went hand in hand. See how these two Christians loved one another!

But notwithstanding this disparity in age,

and even in some respects the lack of mental idiosyncrasy,—work, holy work in the Church of their Great Lord, bound them together. On that multiform and diverse work, we cannot now enter. Timothy seems to have shared, not only the hardships, and dangers, and opposition encountered by his illustrious compeer, but to have participated also in his triumphs. What part he had in the conversions of this Roman capital, we are not informed; but it is worthy of note, that in St Paul's second Epistle to him, noble members of the Church send, at the close, their special salutations; and among these, Pudens and *Claudia*,—the latter name one of special interest to us, as being that of the daughter of a British king; the only name belonging to our country which occurs in sacred history, but the first of the many women of Britain who have since sustained the faith, and helped on the work of God's faithful ministers.*

---

* See Introductory Chapter, p. 55. It has been well observed that, independent of the tie of affection and friendship, it would seem as if some peculiar official connection subsisted between St Paul and Timothy, linking them together as colleagues and

The special centre, however, of Timothy's labours was, not Rome but Ephesus; at that time the greatest city of Asia Minor, and which almost divided with this imperial metropolis a world-wide renown. Here, this young and faithful Evangelist was left to contend, almost single-handed, with the many adverse and baneful influences which surrounded him. His undertaking ministerial duty there, was in itself a beautiful evidence and attestation of his unselfish willingness, in all things, and at all times, to acquiesce in the proposals of his spiritual guide. "I besought thee," says St Paul,

---

copartners in the Church of that age : " Timotheus, my workfellow" (Rom. xvi. 21). Not to speak of the previous Epistles to the Thessalonians, we find the two names occurring, in this conjoint form, in the three letters sent from Rome by St Paul to Philippi, Colosse, and to Philemon. In the first, the initiatory address is " Paul and Timothy, the servants of Jesus Christ." In the other two, the mention of the name of the elder Apostle is followed by "and Timothy our brother." It has been further remarked, by the same discriminating writer, when in one of these letters (that to the Colossians) the name of Luke occurs, who was the most constant companion of St Paul (more frequently with him than even Timothy was), it is not thus conjoined with his in the prefix, but simply occurs towards the end, as sending a message of love to the brethren.—*See Dr Howson's* "*Companions of St Paul*," p. 284.

"to abide at Ephesus." That expression of the great Apostle's wishes was enough; he accepted, without remonstrance or hesitation, the responsibilities of the arduous post. His now aged father in the faith seemed, however, keenly alive to the perils of his new position, and his inadequacy in his own strength and from a constitutional timidity, to combat them. These were partly without, and partly within, the Ephesian Church. Outside, there was the intellectual pride and cunning sophistries of its pagan philosophers,—"the opposition of science falsely so called." There was the religious intolerance and mercenary spirit of the vast multitude of priests and votaries and craftsmen connected with the temple of Diana. There were the subtle arts of the practised magicians and sorcerers. There was the still fiercer bigotry and hate of the Jews, who had numerously settled in this vast emporium of Eastern commerce, and found it a lucrative field for amassing their sordid gains. Then, within the Church, there was the danger, with some, of being contaminated with surrounding worldliness—the prevailing flippancy and voluptuousness of social and fashionable life; with others, there was the risk of giving way to doctrinal defection; with others, of being involved in miserable party factions, or in those controversial disputes which stirred up that "wrath of man which worketh not the righteousness of God." "O Timothy, keep that which is committed to thy trust." "Hold fast the form of sound words which thou hast heard of me in faith and love, which is in Christ Jesus." "For God has not given us the spirit of fear, but of power and love, and of a sound mind."

Whether Timothy was able fully to profit by the warnings and teachings of his faithful monitor,—to resist this flood of evil, and to prove an example "in word, in conversation, in charity, in spirit, in faith, in purity,"—we cannot tell. We have little to guide us in forming an estimate of his later life and labours. Let us, at all events, cherish the hope, that these were in harmony with his antecedent history and character; that he lived not unworthy of his godly parentage; of the prayers which had hovered over his infant couch, and which had followed him from the city of his early habitation ; of the blissful and hallowed companionship which had moulded him in after years, and which had given, in his case, an emphasis to the Psalmist's words, which perhaps they never had before or since : "I am a companion of them that fear Thee." There is strong reason to surmise, that at some time or other, although the period is indeterminate, he had been called to submit to a similar cross with his aged father and friend, by wearing the chains of captivity. This we infer from St Paul's incidental reference at the close of his Epistle to the Hebrews, " Know ye that our brother Timothy is *set at liberty*." Indeed, some imagine, the reference is to a share of the great Apostle's first imprisonment at Rome, and that it was before the same terrible tribunal he himself was soon to be sisted, that he charged ' his son' to witness a good confession, even as their adorable Master, in the presence of Pilate, had done before them. (1 Tim. vi. 12, 13.)

We need not attempt to trace farther, Timothy's work and career. And as to his latter end, we can only accept, for what it is worth, the testimony of tradition, that on the occasion of a great festival to Diana, in which he endeavoured to raise his protesting voice, he was made a victim to the fury of the fanatic mob, who dispatched him with clubs, close to the gigantic temple of the goddess, and that his body was brought subsequently to Rome.

We love better to think of him (as already described, in relation to the subject we are now pursuing), as the Apostle's latest, fastest, dearest friend. Previous to St Paul's imprisonment, they seem to have taken a mutual parting, under an impression that they would never meet again. The faithful son of such an affectionate father had wept bitterly at the thought of seeing his face no more—" I thank God, whom I serve from my forefathers with pure conscience, that without ceasing I have remembrance of thee in my prayers night and day; greatly desiring to see thee, *being mindful of thy tears*, that I may be filled with joy" (2 Tim. i. 3, 4). But God had still spared him. They may yet meet again. The spirit of the old man, like another Jacob, revives, with the hope, that he who had so " fully known his afflictions" in the past (2 Tim. iii. 10), who had been so thoroughly cognisant of fifteen long years of varying tribulation, would be with him when entering the shadows of the dark valley. Timothy was far distant in Asia; but St Paul, as we have seen, earnestly urges him to come with all speed. Yet, owing to the many dangers around, fearing lest even he might be deterred from giving his dying sympathy, he exhorts him to boldness in the cause of Jesus in this most beautiful letter—the second Epistle. Time forbids us to pause and analyse its touching contents. It bears in its postscript, "Written from Rome, when Paul was brought before Nero the second time." We may well regard it as the farewell *souvenir* of a loving friendship; quite what we would have expected from the pen of one, conscious that he might probably be writing his last words. It reminds us of the ray which often bursts out before a troubled sunset, shooting athwart the whole landscape. The Apostle's memory, like that parting gleam, retraverses the long years of a cherished attachment, and lives them in thought over again. He begins with the scenes of childhood at Lystra; a parent's hallowed home; their mutual prayers, and faith, and tears; Timothy's public consecration to the ministry; his unfaltering adherence to himself; the persecutions he endured; following up, with solemn, searching counsels, such as a faithful and beloved dying friend alone would use;—one who felt that the moments were fleeting,—that he had but few words to say, and a brief time to utter them. "What mother," says the sainted Monod, "ever wrote to her son a letter more full of solicitude?" The sentence at the close, "*Grace be with you, Amen,*" was probably the last his trembling hand traced.

We can well imagine how these dying exhortations and benedictions would be treasured in hallowed and enduring remembrance. What could be a nobler stimulus to this young soldier of the cross, to fight manfully the battles of truth, than the closing unflinching testimony—the triumphant dying experience, of him whom he regarded with such reverence and love? Would it not brace and support him for a similar hour? That dauntless apostle could tell, how when "all men forsook him," "notwithstanding, the Lord stood with him and strengthened him." He could leave, as his dying watchword, a sacred bequest to all similarly called to witness by suffering for the truth: "And the Lord *shall* deliver me from every evil work, and will preserve me unto His heavenly kingdom." And yet, observe, even when he speaks to Timothy of his readiness for departure, and of the crown of life promised to the faithful unto death, he casts every gem of that crown at the feet of Him who is "THE LORD HIS RIGHTEOUSNESS." The theme of his life lingers on his lips when about to soar amid ministering seraphim. What heroic confidence, yet what childlike humility, are in these words, penned amid the gloom of his Roman dungeon!—" I am now ready to be offered, and the time of my departure is at hand: I have fought a good fight, I have finished my course, I have kept the faith; henceforth there is laid up for me a crown of RIGHTEOUSNESS, which the Lord, the righteous Judge, shall give me at that day."

I repeat, could Timothy forget these words when the moment of his own departure came? Would they not be like an angel whispering to him? Would they not prove like a rod and staff amid the swellings of Jordan?

Be this as it may, we can at all events think of the younger Apostle, now seated by his spiritual Father, among the honoured band of those who have "turned many to righteousness:" the companionship, intermitted for a few stormy years on earth, resumed, never to be broken, in the general assembly and Church of the first-born in Heaven!

May we too, in a humbler sense, share in this blissful and honoured association. There can indeed be no possible identity of experience between us and these two sainted men. The times of suffering and martyrdom are, thank God, for the present over; the dungeons of bigotry are for the present closed; the sword of persecution slumbers in its scabbard. But let us seek to imitate them in the lowlier virtues of the everyday Christian character; let us follow them in their faith and love, and in the ceaseless activities of a consecrated life; that thus, when we too come to sleep the last sleep,—not amid the glow of lamps which superstition burns around emblazoned altars,—but wherever our ashes repose (be it amid the quiet seclusion of the old village churchyard at home, where memory keeps ever sacred vigil over the loved and lost), it may be ours, though with infinitely lowlier claims, to covet, as the noblest of epitaphs—that which now in golden letters gleams over the double shrine with which all here are familiar—"TO ME TO LIVE IS CHRIST, AND TO DIE IS GAIN."

SERMON IV.

The Bible in Rome. St Paul's Roman Testimony to its Inspiration. The Word of God not Bound.

"And that from a child thou hast known THE HOLY SCRIPTURES, WHICH ARE ABLE TO MAKE THEE WISE UNTO SALVATION THROUGH FAITH WHICH IS IN CHRIST JESUS. ALL SCRIPTURE IS GIVEN BY INSPIRATION OF GOD, and is profitable for doctrine, for reproof, for correction, for instruction in righteousness: that the man of God may be perfect, throughly furnished unto all good works."—2 TIM. iii. 15–17.

"But the Word of God is not bound."—2 TIM. ii. 9.

"And when they had appointed him a day, there came many to him into his lodging; to whom he expounded and testified the kingdom of God, persuading them concerning Jesus, both out of the law of Moses, and out of the prophets, from morning till evening."—ACTS xxviii. 23.

IV.

(Preached at the Porta del Popolo, March 12, 1871.)*

2 TIM. iii. 15, 16.

"The Holy Scriptures, which are able to make thee wise unto salvation through faith which is in Christ Jesus. All Scripture is given by inspiration of God."

LAST Lord's Day, I directed your thoughts to that sacred relation in which St Paul stood to Timothy, and the hallowed memories, alike scriptural and traditional, in regard to both, which hover over this city.

There is much in the great Apostle's letters to his son in the faith, and especially in the later one, penned in his Roman dungeon, of

---

* It was a remarkable coincidence, that the very time I was engaged in preaching this sermon in Rome, several thousands of the new National Guard of King Victor Emanuel were being sworn in; and the oath of allegiance was taken, not (as had been the immemorial custom), with the hand laid on the crucifix, but on the Holy Bible. Two copies of the Scriptures were placed open on a table; the Jews took their oath on the Old Testament, the Christians on the Old and New together.

momentous practical import. There would seem to be a special appropriateness, at this time and in this place, in selecting for consideration, among its other themes, St Paul's testimony to the divine obligation of the Holy Scriptures. We have surely arrived at a wonderful juncture and crisis of ROME'S history, when, after centuries of proscription, that blessed Book is once more free to enter within its gates—when God's ambassadors can unlock its long-sealed fountains, and without let or hindrance can proclaim, " Ho, every one that thirsteth, come ye to the waters!" On receiving the crowd of inquirers in "his own hired house," it was from these Sacred Scriptures, during the livelong day, the Apostle enforced the claims of his great mission; for we read, "there came many to him into his lodging, to whom he expounded and testified the kingdom of God ; persuading them concerning Jesus, both out of *the law of Moses, and out of the prophets*, from morning till evening" (Acts xxviii. 23). It was these Sacred Scriptures, as God's own honoured instrumentality in the world's conversion, which gave comfort to the chained prisoner himself, as he looked to his bonds, and thought for a moment with sadness of the arrest thus put upon his labours: "I suffer trouble as an evil-doer, even unto bonds; but *the Word of God* is not bound." He could then verify words he had inserted in his letter to the Church in Rome, long before he had personally set foot within the city, "Whatsoever things were written aforetime were written for our learning, that we through patience and comfort of *the Scriptures* might have hope" (Rom. xv. 4). It was with these Sacred Scriptures, as with the Sword of the Spirit, Timothy was to fight the battles of the faith as his great spiritual father had before him—" I charge thee, therefore, before God and the Lord Jesus Christ, who shall judge the quick and the dead at His appearing and His kingdom, preach *the Word*." When he exhorted him to be a workman, needing not to be ashamed, it was by "rightly dividing *the Word of truth;*" and through these Sacred Scriptures, as the man of God, he was to be " perfect, thoroughly furnished."

There are few themes, moreover, which, at the

present period, demand more earnest and faithful handling. We cannot close our eyes to the fact, that, in varied ways and under specious pretexts, not a few are tempted, in these times of rampant and reckless speculation, to tamper with the authority of God's Word, and are thereby digging a mine underneath their feet. By a surrender of their old child-like belief in its inspired utterances, they are making "shipwreck of faith." That of "a good conscience" may speedily follow. For alas! there is too often a fatal connection—that of cause and effect—between the infidelity of the head and the infidelity of the heart. Considering, as British Protestants, that the Bible is the most precious of inheritances, it may not be unsuitable that I refresh your memories, not with any new truths, but with a few old and familiar thoughts on the Inspiration of the Holy Scriptures;—the obligation laid on us to search them, and to value them as the very Oracles of God. They have made every Christian, and every Christian nation, what they are. May the Holy Spirit vouchsafe us His presence and blessing.

The words I have read as a text, embrace manifold topics. Let us limit ourselves to three.

I. The statement regarding the inspiration of the sacred Volume, "*All Scripture is given by inspiration of God.*"

II. The design of the Holy Scriptures, "*which are able to make wise unto salvation.*"

III. The medium by which this is effected, "*Through faith which is in Christ Jesus.*"

I. What do we mean by *Inspiration?* Inspiration is literally "a breathing into." There was a divine, God-breathing;* a supernatural influence brought to bear on the souls of the writers. So that what was dictated to them, and written by them, was the very mind of Deity. St Peter says, "The prophecy came not in old time by the will of man, but holy men of God spake as they were moved by the Holy Ghost." It was not they who spake, but the Spirit speaking in them and by them.

And here the words of St Paul written from

---

* "θεόπνευστος."

Rome to Timothy, lead me specially to observe (as meeting one more recent and prevalent phase of modern infidelity), that the Old and New Testament are of equally binding obligation. There are those who assent to the inspiration and authority of the latter, who would reject and repudiate that of the former,—those very Scriptures to which the Apostle in the text alone could refer;—for, I need not say, it must have been with the writings of Moses and the Prophets, and the Psalms, that Timothy's grandmother Lois and his mother Eunice stored his young and susceptible mind in the early home at Lystra. Observe, St Paul here makes the remarkable statement, that these ancient oracles (independent of the augmentation they were to receive from his own inspired utterances, and, above all, from the four Gospels, containing the words and sayings of the Great Master) were "able to make wise unto salvation." These Old Testament Scriptures, you do not require to be told, are constantly alluded to in the course of the New, not only by the Evangelists themselves and the other sacred penmen, but, what is more to us, they are also frequently, in the form of quotations, cited by the lips of the Lord of evangelists. In the mysterious years of that divine youth and boyhood—in the quiet nurture and training of His Nazareth home, or amid the deep seclusion of its surrounding green hills and valleys, He seems to have garnered His divine-human memory with these holy treasures, many portions of which were in due time to receive a new and higher consecration, if this were possible, by being among the "gracious words which proceeded out of His mouth." Again and again does He make reference to the entire canon of the Old Testament as "the Word of God:" moreover, investing it, as the arbiter in all questions, with peerless authority. He honours it; fulfils it; yields to it unquestioning submission; sets upon its inspired utterances His *imprimatur* and seal. Even in one of His parables, though He puts the saying in the lips of father Abraham, yet in reality it is His own, —" If they hear not *Moses and the prophets*, neither will they be persuaded though one rose from the dead." When He confronts the father of lies in the hour of the desert temptation, what were His weapons? They were taken from the same armoury. Thrice He spurns back the tempter, by an appeal to the Old Testament Scriptures, "*It is written.*" To the money-changers, carrying on their flagitious traffic in the temple-courts, He delivers the withering rebuke, "*It is written*, My house shall be called an house of prayer, but ye have made it a den of thieves." When, in the lowly Galilean village of which we have just spoken, He commenced His ministry, what were the opening words He selected as His text? As if He wished, in this interesting hour of His great mission, to stamp His own signature on Old Testament scripture, He takes into His hand the holy writings, and reads from the prophet Isaiah, "The Spirit of the Lord is upon me, because the Lord hath anointed me to preach glad tidings to the meek:" and when the eyes of all in the synagogue were fastened on Him, He says, "This day is this Scripture fulfilled in your ears." Step by step in His mysterious pilgrimage of love, in instances too numerous to dwell upon, He seems consumed with zeal to fulfil the sayings of Holy Writ; for it is always added, He did such and such things, "that it might be fulfilled which was spoken." With the Scripture, He braced Himself for His cross and passion : "He took the twelve aside, and said, Behold we go up to Jerusalem, that *all things which are written* may be accomplished." Old Testament quotations were among His last expiring utterances. Perhaps more remarkable still, when the risen Conqueror met His disciples at Gennesaret, and they partook of their simple feast on its strand, it is the fulfilment of the Hebrew Scriptures which seems uppermost in his heart: "These are the words which I spake unto you while I was yet with you, that all things must be fulfilled which were written in the law of Moses, and in the prophets, and in the Psalms concerning me. Then opened He their understandings that they might understand *the Scriptures*." Daring intellectual pride, captious questionings, may well be rebuked, when we mark the estimate thus put upon these sacred oracles by Him who was

Truth incarnate. He never regarded them as the fabulous legends of an early age, a worn-out Book, which the world and the Church in wiser times can lay aside. He never considered some portions as inspired and some not—like the statue of Nebuchadnezzar, partly of iron and partly of clay. No! it is an entire Volume. He interjects in one of His discourses the remarkable assertion, "The Scripture cannot be broken." Every link of this golden chain was sacred and necessary for the strength and cohesion of the rest. No stone of the divine edifice can be wanting. Like His own garment, these divine words are one,—"woven without seam throughout from the top to the bottom." Well, surely, may we love the Book He loved, read the Book He read, trust the Book He trusted, honour the Book He honoured; which comforted Him in His sorrows, and supported Him in His strong temptations, and with whose utterances on His tongue He breathed away His spirit. He taught its truths, He sang its hymns, He prayed its prayers, He drank its solaces. It is a souvenir of the Great Master.

It wears on its every page His image and superscription. The footsteps of the Lord of glory are there, and no tidal wave of irreverent modern criticism and infidelity can sweep them away.

Another question suggests itself. It is here said, "*All* Scripture is given by inspiration of God." What is the extent of that "*all?*"

In answering that question, we must carefully guard ourselves from any misapprehension, by the employment of phrases having an ambiguous meaning. But we shall not be misunderstood when we affirm, that, in the generally accepted use of the term, the theory of minute "verbal inspiration" seems now, with common consent, to be abandoned. In other words, the sacred writers seem to have been left to clothe the divine communications in their own garb. Isaiah has his own elevated dramatic imagery, Jeremiah his plaintiveness, Ezekiel his reiterations, Nahum and Habakkuk their vehement rushing numbers; while in the New Testament, John and Luke, Paul and James and Peter, all similarly retain their peculiar style, phraseology, and idiomatic expressions. They were not tied down to mere words. They were not mere passive machines in the hands of the Great Inspirer. Hence, too, we see that the narratives of the Gospels, though giving substantially the same facts, clothe these in different language, and describe them from different stand-points. The writers were each and all *divinely* inspired, and yet they were *human* agents. The inspiration did not cancel their humanity, neither did their humanity eclipse the divinity of their record. In stating this, there is a beautiful analogy often employed between the written Word (the Scripture) and Him who is called the *Word of God*, the Man, Christ Jesus. In His case (to use the theological phrase), we have the hypostatical union of the two natures in the one Person. He was *Divine*, yet *human*. The real humanity did not detract from the reality of His Godhead, yet neither did the Godhead and supreme Divinity diminish the actuality of His manhood. He was the great Jehovah, the Creator of all worlds; yet He was true *Man*, in all His feelings and sympathies and innocent infirmities, though in these absolutely faultless. So with the written Word. It is *divine;* it is the declaration of God's own sacred, unchanging mind to His Church. But it finds its way through human instrumentality. The voice is from heaven; the river, clear as crystal, is from before the throne; but the channel through which it flows, with its windings and scenery, is all human. The golden oil of the candlestick is distilled from above, from the two everlasting Olive-trees; but the pipes which convey it to feed the lamps are human, and may vary in shape, and size, and lustre (Zech. iv. 2, 3). Hence there may be diversities of gifts and temperaments in the writers; the verbal narratives of the Evangelists may vary; there may be apparent discrepancies in these tints in the divine picture; but the mind of God is faithfully conveyed notwithstanding. Each inspired historian can say with David, " My tongue is the pen of a ready writer,"—that ready Writer being the Spirit of God. " Holy men of God spake," but yet (to repeat the assertion of St Peter, already quoted) they "spake as they were moved by the Holy Ghost." We have "not the words which man's wisdom teacheth, but which the Holy Ghost teacheth." * That Bible would be incomprehensible on the theory of mere human authorship. Many of its writers, the compositors of this great repertory of divine life and love and consolation, were illiterate, uneducated men,—strangers to all the learning and culture of the schools. They were separated from one another by hundreds, indeed thousands of years. And yet what a unity in their books! Peasants, Herdsmen, Pilgrims, Fishermen, Shepherds, Vine-dressers, Physicians, Lawgivers, Philoso-

---

* This is well put in the words of an excellent writer and theologian: "As a skilful musician, called to execute alone some masterpiece, puts his lips by turns to the mournful flute, the shepherd's reed, the mirthful pipe, and the war trumpet; so the Almighty God, to sound in our ears His eternal Word, has selected from of old, the instruments best suited to receive successively the breath of His Spirit. Thus we have in God's great Anthem of Revelation, the sublime simplicity of John, the elliptical, soul-stirring energy of St Paul, the fervour and solemnity of St Peter, the poetic grandeur of Isaiah, the lyric moods of David, the ingenuous and majestic narratives of Moses, the sententious and royal wisdom of Solomon. Yes, it was all this; it was Peter, Isaiah, Matthew, John, and Moses, but it was God" (Gaussen).

phers, Priests, Kings. And what diversity of subjects! Psalms, Prophecies, Canticles, Proverbs, Laws, Ethics, Biography, History, Letters. Yet what concord, homogeneity! and that too without the possibility of collusion, or preconcerted plan. The Temple with one Altar and one God, yet with a thousand windows all shedding the same mellowed divine light. They have weaved one beautiful, consistent pattern, one harmonious whole. They point to one and the same glorious method of salvation, and one too beyond the ken of human reason. "Built upon the foundation of Apostles and Prophets," we have here a building "fitly framed together." It is more than man's work. It points to its own high original. It bears the seal and signature of Heaven.

How wonderfully, too, has God preserved the Bible amid surrounding error and corruption, causing it to come down unmutilated and uninjured, and to float like a sacred ark in the midst of the waters. No Book has been in such jeopardy. And no wonder; for its precepts are so holy; in this respect presenting such a contrast with the impure systems of Pagan religion and philosophy,—the mythologies of Greece and Rome, the Shasters of the Brahmin, the writings of Confucius, and the Koran of Mahomet. Running counter to all the corruptions of fallen humanity, it yet still outlives all assaults. The philosophic pen of Gibbon assailed it; the polished shafts of Bolingbroke; the subtlety of Mirabeau and Rousseau; the blasphemy of Voltaire. The bush has burned with fire, but the living God is in the bush, and therefore it is not consumed. So that we can say of His *Word*, what the Psalmist said of His Works in the firmament of heaven, "They continue this day according to Thine ordinance, for all are Thy servants."

II. Let me pass now, in the second place, to note, in the text, the *object* of the Scriptures: "*Which are able to make thee wise unto salvation.*" In reading a book, we either have, or ought to have, its object in view. We do not look to it for information on foreign or extraneous subjects. We are content if each writer handles, ably and well, the matter on hand. How many a querulous and captious mind would reject the Bible as not inspired, because its writers have not anticipated the discoveries of modern science, or because, in some embarrassing phrases, they seem to run counter to its conclusions and deductions. We answer,—The Bible was not written to be an authority, or book of reference, on cosmical subjects; to instruct on geological epochs and primary strata, nor to anticipate the philosopher—the High priest of nature—in the discovery of those great laws which regulate alike the formation of the raindrop, and the revolution of the planets. It was written, not to solve physical problems, but to "make wise unto salvation." Moreover, even when Science and Revelation are apparently in antagonism, it is our duty not precipitately to accept, by any rash induction, plausible theories, until these are fully tested and confirmed. With the profoundest reverence for our great explorers of nature, we have had experience that oracular responses from the Temple of science are not to be received, in all cases, as final and infallible, and that what sometimes has been boldly inserted in the category of ascertained data, has been nullified and negatived by subsequent discoveries. "He that believeth in this, as in more important things, should 'not make haste.'" Nay, more; we make bold to say, there is no such real and formidable antagonism, as is often alleged, between science and inspiration. Some of the most distinguished votaries of the former have received, with the simplicity and docility of children, the lessons of the sacred page. They have attested, alike in their living and in their dying hours, that (to use the words of one of the master intellects of the age) "the most daring speculations as to nature, may be accompanied with the humblest faith in those sublime doctrines, that open Heaven alike to the wisest philosopher and to the simplest peasant."

My brethren, let us look to this blessed Bible as a great *personal* blessing. I am warranted to each individual here to say, 'It is a message from God *to thee.*' It is the very message you need. It comes home to the great heart of humanity. How it speaks to the conscience! What a discerner of the moral being! Like the wheels of Ezekiel's vision, it is "full of eyes before and behind." How it ransacks the halls of memory; penetrates the labyrinths of the soul;—a faithful mirror reflecting and exposing the chambers of imagery. And then, when it brings you and me as poor, helpless, needy, condemned, lost, to yearn after some 'Daysman' to 'lay his hand upon us both,' it presents us with the object of our search. It meets the longing necessities of our natures—"Believe in the Lord Jesus Christ, and thou shalt be saved." It offers us a complete salvation; a salvation not only from the guilt, but from the power of sin. It comes to us, independent of all churches and conventional distinctions. It meets us on the common ground of humanity; as sinners carrying the same burdens, subject to the same weaknesses, grappling with the same temptations, bowed with the same sorrows, travelling to the same goal of death, having the same reversion of an eternal destiny. Never book spake like this

Book. You can say of it, as David of Goliath's sword, " There is none like it." It is a volume suited for all, designed for all;—young and old, rich and poor, learned and unlearned. In the well-known words of Tertullian, " It is like a great lake, in which some places are so deep that an elephant may swim in them, and other parts so shallow that a child can wade through them." And, last of all, it opens, as no other Revelation ever did, or ever can, the gates into the Celestial City. It is a glorious fiery pillar, lighting the van of the true Israel of God through every stage of the journey, till it brings them to the heavenly Canaan. And is not this an object worthy of the Great Father of all?—to prepare this missive of love for His sin-stricken, diseased, captive, dying children; that with it in their hands as an infallible directory and guide, they may go up and on through the wilderness to the Eternal Home, gladdened with hopes which are full of immortality!

III. Let us note, finally, the *way* or *medium* by which the Scriptures make wise unto salvation. It is "*through faith which is in Christ Jesus.*" The whole plan of salvation is therein clearly revealed, but we require to put forth the hand of faith to appropriate and make it our own. The Divine Word contains the remedy; but you must apply it *by faith*, if you would experience the healing power. And it is "through faith which is *in Christ Jesus.*" To Him the Scriptures ever point. It was His own assertion, when unfolding the work of the Holy Spirit—the Inspirer of these sacred penmen, " He shall glorify ME, for He shall receive of mine, and shall show it unto you." To Him every street in this Bible city conducts, as its Great Centre. John's exclamation forms the key-note to all the music of the inspired canon with its varying harmonies, " Behold the Lamb of God!" "This is *the* record, that God hath given to us eternal life, and this life is in His Son." It is not likely that I address any such on this occasion, but if there be even one here, in this sceptic age, who may have been hitherto a neglecter of his Bible,—perhaps secretly calling in question its verity as an inspired Book,—I would say, "Go, read that Bible; not with a querulous, captious, cavilling spirit, warped and biassed with foregone conclusions, seeking only to find fault, and to discover flaws and blemishes; but read it "as you would a letter from the father you love in a distant land;" read it with a candid, honest, open, unprejudiced, child-like mind, and you will find it contains the very message and the very salvation your needy soul requires: "The *meek* will He guide in judgment, and the meek will He teach His way." We do not undervalue the external evidences of the Bible's genuineness and authenticity; but we dwell much on the *subjective* evidence. It addresses itself to the heart. It discovers its secret maladies. It offers a blessed panacea and cure for its deepest wounds and most inveterate ailments. It only asks us to test their efficacy by immediate application: "If any man will do (or *willeth* to do) His will, he shall know of the doctrine whether it be of God"—"The entrance of Thy Word giveth light, it giveth understanding to the simple." You will be best certified that this is the true light by admitting it, the true bread by eating it, the living water by drinking it. To adopt, in substance, the simple but apposite illustration of a great modern champion of the faith :—"Suppose a heavenly canopy was let down from the sky on the earth ; that there were protuberances here and there on the earth's surface, and that this supernal canopy exactly fitted these, what would you infer? Would it not be that He who made that canopy knew all the earth;—in other words, that he was God? The Bible is that canopy, which He lets down on the human heart. Who can doubt that the Creator of the heart was the Author of the Book."* See how it fits it! how it speaks to your deepest experience, telling you all things that ever you did! See how it rebukes your corruptions! See how it addresses you (as you feel yourselves to be), guilty, helpless sinners in His sight! See how it imparts mysterious peace,—tells you of a Friend, a Saviour, a Sanctuary, a Heaven! See how it points to rest for the weary, a home for the pro-

---

* *Dr Chalmers' Evidences of Christianity.*

digal, salvation for the lost! How these great words of comfort, in prophecy and psalm, which Timothy possessed—how these Gospels and Epistles which have been bequeathed to the Church since his day, have from their storehouses of consolation and promise dried your tears when you have sat by the deathbed, or come broken-hearted from the grave! Could this be the book of impostors? Could this have been written by designing men? Could this be a lie of the Jews of Palestine, or of the priesthood of the Middle Ages, palmed on the credulous? Could this be any other book than the Book of God? Oh! in our times of sorrow, sickness, death, "if these foundations were destroyed, what would the righteous do?"

And then, let me ask again, if there be any here (I hope not), drifting out in the infinite of darkness, to whom I can put the question—Has infidelity solved for you the great problems of aching humanity? Has it moored you to a safe and peaceful anchorage? Has it spoken the needed "Peace, be still!" to your tempest-tossed spirit? You are advancing year by year, day by day, nearer eternity; and when you take at last that infinite *leap*, where will you alight? Alas! you know not. Go and test for yourselves, by a faithful and reverential perusal of God's Holy Word, whether we are only mocking you with idle tales, when we speak of it as offering a safe—the only safe footing. But *have* you read it? I find that is the pertinent question put by a faithful servant of God, who himself once sat in the seat of the scorner. Speaking from his own experience, he well adds, that the most unreasonable and unphilosophical of all sceptics are those who reject this Book of books, yet who have never almost opened it—never examined the testimony they despise. "Read, read the Bible," said Wilberforce on his deathbed; "through all my perplexities I never read any other book, and I never felt the want of any other." I ask you, moreover, to read it with prayer. Other subjects of study do not require to be mastered thus. Books of history or science need no such divine accompaniment to make them plain. But God has told us that the veil of the heart—the veil of unbelief and prejudice—must be rent away. Prayer is the hand which removes the obstruction. Prayer is the sacred ploughshare which lays open the furrows of the soul for the reception of the heavenly seed. Prayer is the divine telescope which reveals the glories of the inspired firmament. "Open Thou mine eyes that I may behold wondrous things out of Thy law." When the once infidel Lord Lyttelton came to peruse the Scriptures in this teachable, devotional spirit, see how he believed and trembled and rejoiced, and built up the faith which he once sought to destroy; so that he could have been sooner convinced that no sun blazed in the heavens by day, or no moon shed her silvery glory by night, than that this Holy Book and its Author were not divine. Cling to it through life's morning and midday, as the man of your counsel. At life's sunset, let its glorious truths, like the Alpine summits, be illuminated to your spiritual vision when the valleys are in shadow. Be able then to say, with good old Dr Marsh of Beckenham, after a life of lofty consecration, as the glories of the New Jerusalem were dawning upon him—"With this staff have I travelled through my pilgrimage, and with this staff shall I pass through Jordan."

And what this precious Bible has proved to individuals, may it prove (or rather, has it not by God's blessing proved, and will it not still further prove), to nations—to the world? Those kingdoms are now the few exceptions which have not already listened to its sublime messages. Traverse what climes we may, to earth's remotest shores, there is no speech nor language where the voice of the Holy Oracles has not been heard. Their "line is gone to all the earth, and their words unto the end of the world." We behold the Esquimaux and the Laplander in the frigid zone, gazing, through them, on the better Sun of Righteousness. We behold the Gospel Temple gleaming amid the fogs of their eternal winter; we hear the Gospel Anthem chanted by their hardy sons. Under the teachings of Scripture, we behold the slave forgetting his chains, in the consciousness of a freedom of which the tyrant that galls him knows nothing.

We behold the degraded African—the type of mental imbecility, weeping over his Bible, and exulting in the wisdom that cometh down from above. We behold the swarthy Indian of the Far West, hanging the trumpet of war mute on the walls of the Gospel Sanctuary, and, leaning on his reversed spear, listening to this Word of life from the Ambassador of peace. We behold the bloodthirsty cannibal, as he reads the blessed page, shedding tears over the victims of past ferocity, and exulting only in the blood which cleanseth from all sin. We behold, under its unfoldings of a nobler philosophy, the Pagodas of India tottering to their base, and the subtleties of the Hindoo yielding to the sublime simplicities of the faith of Jesus. We behold, through its revelations of the true "Celestial," the Chinese renouncing hereditary superstitions, exulting alone in those walls which are salvation, and those gates which are praise; a response (feeble yet it may be, but which will one day become as the voice of many waters), given to the dying missionary's noble battle-cry—" China for Christ!" Nearer home, we behold Spain—Spain, so rich in material resources,—the country, above all others, on which Nature has poured her bounties with most lavish profusion, rising from the tyranny of ages; and as she claims her place among the nations of "the free," asserting her right also to freedom's best heritage—liberty of conscience, and an unclasped Bible. And, more than all, this ITALY—the most magnificent of earth's inheritances, from the Alps to the Adriatic, can now hear and read the Word of life. We know too well, that while the Apocalyptic Angel, with the little Book in his hand, had, for half a century, winged his way unchallenged to the remotest wilds of heathenism,—to Roman Christendom that everlasting Gospel was an interdicted and forbidden Volume. It is so no longer. Two Bible depôts, as you are aware, are now opened in two of the principal streets in this capital. One of these shared, a few weeks ago, in the common disaster caused by the sudden flooding of the Tiber. But let us accept it, in the old city of omens, rather as the emblem and prophecy of coming blessing, when the Spirit of the Lord shall descend "as floods upon the dry ground," and like the swollen river of Ezekiel's vision (bearing on its bosom the great message of love and mercy), "wherever the river cometh, there shall be life." Yes! the God of the Bible is appearing to stand by the gates of this glorious land, and saying to all Churches and all Bible Societies, "Behold, I have set before you an open door, and no man can shut it."

Who that has visited the recent excavations at the Palatine Hill, can have failed to note that remarkable ilex-tree, whose root and scarred stem, though long buried among the ruins, has not only survived, but survived to rend the old palace walls, and shoot upwards in a mass of living green, overtopping the desolation around? It alone has apparently outlived the Cæsars,—triumphed over the wreck and decay of palatial residences, which their imperial builders deemed to be immortal. May we not take it as a type and symbol of the triumphs in reserve for God's Word, long buried in this country by the apostasy of ages? The day has come when the true

Living Tree has rent the superincumbent walls, and is now sending its roots downwards and its branches upwards, reading the great lesson to the oldest kingdom of the world, in the midst of a city which called itself Eternal—"The grass withereth, the flower fadeth, BUT *the Word of our God shall stand for ever.*" May the leaves of the Tree be more and more for the healing of this nation! May there be many faithful men raised up from among all the true Churches of Christendom, to sound forth, in its midst, the silver tones of this true Trumpet of Jubilee! May there be earnest effort, simple faith, faithful prayer, abundant blessing! May the Lord Himself give the word, and great shall be the company of them that publish it!

SERMON V.

St Paul's Converts in Rome: Among the Soldiers—Among the Poor and Degraded. Onesimus.

"But I would ye should understand, brethren, that the things which happened unto me have fallen out rather unto the furtherance of the Gospel; so that my bonds in Christ are manifest in all the palace, and in all other places."—PHILIP. i. 12, 13.

"Yet, for love's sake, I rather beseech thee, BEING SUCH AN ONE AS PAUL THE AGED, AND NOW ALSO A PRISONER OF JESUS CHRIST. I BESEECH THEE FOR MY SON ONESIMUS, WHOM I HAVE BEGOTTEN IN MY BONDS."—PHILEM. 9, 10.

"With Onesimus, a faithful and beloved brother, who is one of you: they shall make known unto you all things which are done here."—COL. iv. 9.

V.

(Preached at the Porta del Popolo, March 19, 1871.)

PHILEM. 9, 10.

"Being such an one as Paul the aged, and now also a prisoner of Jesus Christ. I beseech thee for my son Onesimus, whom I have begotten in my bonds."

ON a recent Sabbath, I spoke of St Paul's confidential friends—the sacred fellowships he enjoyed in ROME, and more especially his main friendship, that of Timothy.

It would be interesting for us to know all the history of these two long and eventful years in his "hired house;" the intercourse he held with brethren and congenial associates; the influence the great man must have exercised over the minds of the very soldiers to whom he was chained, similar to the kindred marvellous influence we find him wielding among the sailors in the Sea of Adria. In the case of such prisoners as he, it was the custom for the soldier on guard to be relieved frequently, if not daily. We may imagine therefore, in the course of "two whole years," how many such sentinels would have the privilege of seeing and hearing the "ambassador in bonds;" listening at times, as he dictated to his amanuensis, those beautiful Epistles, written not for individual Churches alone, but for the ages; or, more frequently, being auditors of his conversation and arguments with the crowds who, it would seem, flocked to his dwelling, and were permitted to hold with him the freest intercourse, "no man forbidding them."* How many would go back, night by night, or day by day, to their barracks to retail the story of this singular captive; his boldness, and earnestness, and ardour—qualities of all others most likely to enlist their interest and commendation! Among that mass of diverse human hearts, the Gospel would doubtless

---

* See this admirably stated by Dean Howson in his "Companions of St Paul," p. 225.

manifest the same varied results it has always displayed, either as "the savour of life unto life," or "of death unto death." Some of these soldiers would return to the Prætorium, or Campus Martius, mocking; others marvelling; others (as we know) believing. Yes, and doubtless these latter would be doomed to undergo the same scoffing and ridicule on the part of their unsympathising comrades, which the British officer or private who avows himself a soldier of the cross, has too often to do at this day. Is it not more than probable that it was these believing sentinels in the Apostle's lodging, who had listened to his wondrous tale of God's love in Christ, who would prove the most effective instruments in the spread of the truths of the Gospel? In a military capital like that of Rome, we can well imagine what a power would be exercised by those of its soldiers who had espoused the Christian faith. Not only would this be the case while quartered within the city itself, but in their foreign campaigns, would they not become the most effective pioneers of the missionary, in carrying tidings of

the new religion to these distant lands?* There
is a surmise, on the part of some writers, that
St Paul himself may have reached the shores of
Britain, and proclaimed the Gospel to its savage
hordes. More likely is it at this time, when we
know the armies of Rome were planting their
eagles in the fens of Norfolk, Cambridge, and
Huntingdon, and on the towers of Colchester,
St Albans, and London, that some of those
very soldiers who, but lately, had had their
hands chained to his in the hired house by the
Tiber, may have carried the glad tidings received from his lips, and proclaimed them by
the banks of the Cam, the Stour, and the
Thames. So that, in accordance with his own
words, which have formed part of our reading
to-day, his "bonds in Christ" were known not
only "in all the Palace (or Prætorian barracks
as that rather means), but *in all other places.*" †

---

* " Companions of St Paul," p. 228.

† No memorial of these early years of the Christian era was so
impressive to me, as that wonderful *Graphite*, now to be seen in
Rome, in the College of the Jesuits (Collegio Romano). Painful, indeed, and repelling it is, in its blasphemy, but valuable
beyond measure as a testimony to the Deity of Christ. In com-

We may probably, in our next, come to speak of the effects of St Paul's presence and preaching on the higher ranks in the Roman capital, reaching even to the inmates of the Imperial Palace.

pany with a distinguished archæologist, I had visited the spot in the Imperial Barracks, on the south substructions of the Palatine, upon whose plaster-wall this rude drawing of about a foot oblong had been discovered. On being admitted to see the fragment itself, I made as careful a copy of it as I could. I confess, so revolting is the treatment of the most sacred of all subjects, that I hesitated considerably before incorporating it in this note. But it supplies such a wonderful indirect evidence to the great foundation-truth of the Christian system, that I have deemed it well to waive these scruples, and subjoin it thus, in a

very diminutive form. It consists, as will at once be seen, of a rude representation of the crucifixion. The Saviour is represented on the Cross having the head of an ass; and beneath, or at the side, is the supposed figure of a worshipper, with the inscription, "Alexamenos sebete Theon" ("Alexamenos worships God"). In other words, "See such a God as Alexamenos worships!" It is impossible to pronounce as to the particular era of the Graphite (or, as it is well called, "Graffito Blasphemo"), although undoubtedly it belongs to one of the earlier centuries, and possibly it may be to the first. [By some it is attributed to the reign of Septimius Severus. Garrucci, who appears to have been present at the discovery, places it at the beginning of the third century. See the grounds for this stated in his "*Deux Monuments des Premiers Siècles*," &c., Rome, 1862.] Let us suppose, however (to give vividness

P

But in addition to the probable, or rather the certain influence, which, as we have now described, he exercised on the common soldiers, it is equally interesting to think of the success achieved by

---

to the explanation, without in any way supporting or vindicating so early a date), that it was of the time of St Paul. A soldier (one who had either listened casually to his preaching, or one of those to whom he was chained) had become a convert to Christianity. This converted soldier returns to the Palatine, and relates his new belief to his scoffing comrade. The latter turns the creed of his fellow-soldier into ridicule ; and just in the way that you would expect from a rude, uncultivated heathen, the latter scratches this hideous caricature on the wall of their barrack-room. The apartment is quite a small one, forming one of a row ; this again consisting probably of stables for the horses, as well as guard-chambers for the men. Little did this jeering Pagan dream, that his blasphemous work would be one day dug up as one of the evidences of Christianity, proving, as it does in the most incontestable form, that the early converts believed the great doctrine that that crucified *Man* was none other than GOD. If it occur to any reader as curious, that the inscription of the Graphite is not in Latin, but in Greek, it should be borne in mind that among the Prætorian Guard of those ages there were as many Greeks as Romans. So prevalent was the Greek language, that Paul's own Epistle to the Romans is written in it. The Greek letters under the shocking representation, give surely to the words of the Apostle elsewhere, greater power and significance : " Christ crucified . . . unto *the Greeks foolishness*" (1 Cor. i. 23). I would advise all visitors to Rome to see for themselves this strange but convincing vindication of the Gospel's cardinal truth ; the sceptic soldier's unintentional attestation to "the great mystery of godliness, GOD manifest in the flesh."

him on those occupying a still different position and scale in social life. The distinctive peculiarity of that Gospel he proclaimed, was, that it was a gospel for the *poor;*—the opening proclamation and manifesto of his great Master was this: "To the poor the Gospel is preached." And not only was it a message of mercy to those who were the children of poverty in respect of outer circumstances and condition,—those whose only birthright was worldly penury,—the beggars on the highway or at the gate, stretching forth their hands for the pittance of the passers-by; but still more was it adapted for the many, who combined with this external misery, spiritual degradation; prodigals wallowing alike in physical and moral pollution—the dregs and sweepings of humanity—castaways of crime, drifting along, reckless and unsuccoured, on the world's wide ocean.

Had St Paul encountered any such in Rome? In that lodging of his (be it where it may), had no such outcast from the degraded homes which surrounded him, come to hear those strange and unwonted words of kindness and compassion?

Was there no abandoned child of Israel who may have rushed to the dens of the Trastevere * to screen himself from the penalties of some hideous crime, who may have crept from his concealment to hear the new tidings brought by this chained prisoner from the land of his Fathers?

We have such an instance of the power of the Gospel to reclaim the most worthless and degraded, in the case of ONESIMUS. His story is embodied in one of the most perfect Epistles that was ever written; a pattern of letter-writing; a model of beauty, and tact, and delicate consideration, which we cannot too minutely study, and too studiously imitate. It has been well denominated by an old writer "The polite Epistle." A celebrated letter, distinguished for its terseness and elegance, written by the younger Pliny on a subject precisely identical, has often been brought into comparison with it. But the refined art and courtesy of Christian love trans-

---

* The Trastevere, as we have explained in the Introductory Chapter, formed the residence of the Jews, and corresponded with the modern Ghetto.

scend the pathos even of the cultured Roman.* Ere we proceed to the subject of this unique letter, it may be well to observe in passing, in connection with its great writer, that it affords confirmation of what more than one commentator has noted—the joyous and animated tone which pervades all the Epistles written during his first imprisonment. Whatever might be his outer circumstances, it is evident the illustrious captive himself, the unabashed freeman of Christ, had become no prey to gloominess; on the contrary, that he was possessor of an inner light and peace—an elastic energy of soul, which had

---

* See *Smith's Bible Dictionary*, art. "Ep. to Philemon." In the same article, it is mentioned that the distinguished Lavater preached thirty-nine sermons on the contents of this brief composition. Luther's estimate of it, as quoted by Alford in his Proleg., is eminently characteristic:—"This Epistle showeth a right noble lovely example of Christian love. Here we see how St Paul layeth himself out for the poor Onesimus, and with all his means pleadeth his cause with his Master. . . . Even as Christ did for us with God the Father, thus also doth St Paul for Onesimus with Philemon. For Christ also stripped Himself of His right, and by love and humility enforced the Father to lay aside His wrath and power, and to take us to His grace for the sake of Christ who lovingly pleaded our cause, and with all His heart layeth Himself out for us. For we are all His Onesimi, to my thinking."

its outward expression in cheerful, and even exultant words. To use the language of an able German theologian, "They are effusions of holy joy from the prisoner of the Lord. That to the Ephesians, a circular Epistle to the Churches in and about Ephesus, is a 'song of degrees' set for the Church of Christ. In it, he contemplates with holy ecstasy God's marvel-building, reared of living souls, and growing together, an holy temple in the Lord, as the historical realisation of the mystery of Christ. Hand in hand with this, goes that to the Colossians, which breathes all the heavenly joy of a cross-honoured confessor. . . . In his Philippian Epistle, Paul's heart leaps for joy and cannot be sad. A dozen times and more, the word 'joy' and 'rejoice' occur in it. The Philippian Church—this pearl of his first love (Acts xvi.)—remained his jewel through life. He cheerfully accepted their 'ministering unto his necessities,' and they were also privileged to communicate with his affliction even at Rome. . . . With great joy also he writes to Philemon; all the grace and loveliness of a manly soul breathes its rich perfume through this little letter of Paul, who in his bonds plays merrily on words,* beseeching Philemon to place to his account, as partner, anything which Onesimus (once servant, now a brother) might be indebted to their joint firm of love." †

There are three individuals, three *dramatis personæ* (if I might so speak), who divide the interest of the letter—the *Apostle Paul*, the *householder of Colosse*, and his slave *Onesimus*. To unfold the little we know regarding the latter, we shall group the three together, and endeavour, from the combination, to glean some profitable reflections.

The world, the most civilised portion of it too, was then cursed with slavery; and no country more so than Phrygia, of which Colosse was the capital. You will remember that St Paul, in writing his Epistle to the Colossians, specially instructs the Christians there, as to the mutual

---

* *Onesimus* means "useful" or "profitable." "In time past to thee *unprofitable*, but now *profitable* to thee and to me," ver. 11, 12.

† See *Besser's* "Paulus" *translated by Bultmann*, pp. 94, 95.

duties of masters and servants (or slaves). "Masters," he says, "give unto your slaves that which is just and equal, knowing that ye have also a Master in heaven." "Servants (or slaves) obey in all things your masters according to the flesh, not with eye-service as men-pleasers, but in singleness of heart, fearing God" (iv. 1, iii. 22).. Onesimus stood in that relation to Philemon. We have good reason to believe he was not, as many were, galled by an oppressive yoke of servitude. Nevertheless, with the native inborn yearning after independence and liberty, he took an opportunity of deserting his master. Moreover, to the guilt of desertion, we have evidence from the Epistle, of the greater crime of having robbed him. Whether implying a large plunder, or a petty embezzlement, we cannot say. Rome was of all places, both from its magnitude and dense population, that in which a fugitive could have the best chance of concealment, and of baffling pursuit. Thither accordingly Onesimus, with his nefarious gains, seems to have betaken himself. The slave of Colosse plunged into the lowest abyss of society, an abyss of which we can form some idea from our knowledge of the lamentable lower strata in our own modern cities. He was an outlaw alike from God and man.

One link alone still bound him to the possibility of a higher life and better hope. His master had become a Christian: he had probably been converted by St Paul. Not unlikely, the Apostle may have visited the house of the wealthy Gentile, on the occasion of his second missionary journey, as he passed through Phrygia,—and there, having been seen by the slave, the latter may have heard from his lips the elements of Christian doctrine. At all events, the two—these extremes of moral and spiritual life, somehow or other, now met at Rome. The pure and noble-minded Paul confronted the debased Onesimus. The name of the former, as I have already said, had doubtless become favourably known among not a few of the humbler classes of the vast capital. They could not understand the religion of Jupiter and Mars, but they could understand and love the touching tale of that Divine Restorer of the suffering and fallen and lost, of whom the Jewish preacher spake—Him who identified Himself with poverty—the reputed carpenter's Son of Nazareth—who, though the foxes had holes, and the birds of the air had nests, had not where to lay His head! As St Paul, in the spirit of his Divine Lord, threw open the doors of his house to "the weary and heavy laden," among that ragged auditory which thronged his dwelling was found ONESIMUS. The grace of God, and the burning words of the prisoner-Apostle, pricked his conscience and melted his heart. The awful sense of his own danger, and of his grievous sins,—doubtless, also, of his ingratitude to an indulgent master, stung him to the quick. What is to be done? Perhaps he had seen enough of St Paul's intercourse with Philemon to feel assured, that he could make the former a safe and reliable confidant of his heart-sorrows and perplexities. He unbosoms to the aged man the strange story of his guilt. Nor is his confidence misplaced. It is a beautiful example, indeed, how (despite of other engrossing anxieties and responsibilities) one individual case could enlist the whole energies of a noble nature. So that, again after the example of the Good Shepherd of the parable, the one footsore and weary wanderer was as dear as the ninety and nine; and it could be said in a lowlier sense of the Apostle, as it was said of a Greater—"He calleth his own sheep by name, and leadeth them out."

But even with such a trusty and powerful intercessor, can Onesimus dream of obtaining Philemon's forgiveness? Never; if his master had been one of the many who manifested no tenderness for their slaves, even when they were obedient, and who would be incapable of exercising mercy or toleration towards runaway thieves. An old writer tells us, "that all owners were looked upon not only by the Roman laws, but by the laws of all nations, as having an unlimited power over slaves. So that without asking the magistrate's leave, or any public or formal trial, they might adjudge them to any work or punishment, even to the loss of life itself." But Onesimus, who had himself felt the subduing, softening power of Christianity, remembered his old master Philemon, as now *the Christian*. It was on this ground alone that St Paul could urge his suit for the extension of pardon and forgiveness, and remove the great burden from the penitent's sensitive heart. This task, it will at once be evident, was encompassed with supreme difficulties, and demanded in its discharge consummate prudence and judgment, touching, as it required to do, from a Christian stand-point, the delicate relation subsisting between slaves and masters. But the Apostle undertakes it; and doubtless undertakes it all the more heartily, as Onesimus, in course of time, under his teaching and training, has become far more than a convert. The once runaway slave has been transformed into a lowly friend and fellow-helper, giving promise of gifts of no ordinary usefulness, which could be turned to special account in the infant Church of the capital.

And this is what first of all strikes us in the letter—the first great lesson which it teaches—it is a lesson we all need constantly to learn and re-learn, that of *unselfishness*. St Paul, as we have just said, clung to Onesimus not only with a personal attachment as a monument of the grace of God (one of the most interesting seals of his ministry and apostleship), but as an auxiliary also in preaching the Gospel, and furthering the great cause of their common Lord. He could ill spare him. But duty was ever with that holy man paramount, and personal considerations subsidiary. He can make no selfish arrangements as to retaining services so valuable, till he get the sanction of Onesimus' master. In a spirit of noble self-denial and deference for the rights of others, he surrenders his own fond wishes and claims. The journey is a long one,—necessarily entailing a period of absence and intermission of labour, which the Apostle would grudge. But there can be no deflection from the path of duty and honourable obligation. Onesimus must personally go back the bearer of this letter. He must confront his old master face to face; and if he return to Rome, he must do so with his full approval. In the letter itself, how touchingly St Paul brings before Philemon, the new relationship which the

Gospel had established between himself and his former slave! He asks (ver. 16), that he be now received back, not as a menial and bondsman, but as "above a servant, nay, as a brother beloved." He assures him, that the kindly sympathy and consideration bestowed on Onesimus, he would accept in the light of a personal boon (ver. 17). "If thou count me therefore a partner, receive him as myself;"—they are all one in Christ Jesus. He even delicately refers to the money-value of the goods of which Philemon had been plundered. The poverty-stricken Apostle does his best to grant, what has been happily called, "a promissory note" for the amount of embezzlement (ver. 18)—"If he have wronged thee, or oweth thee ought, put that on mine account. *I, Paul, have written it with mine own hand, I will repay it.*"

With this letter in hand, Onesimus proceeds to Colosse. We can only imagine what his mingled feelings must have been, in approaching the house of his old master. We cannot doubt the result; though we are not specially informed of it. Both had read the words, "But I say unto you, love your enemies; bless them that curse you, do good to them that hate you, and pray for them that despitefully use you and persecute you; that you may be the children of your Father which is in Heaven." They were now children of that common Father,—members of the one spiritual brotherhood,—and rejoice together in the same liberty wherewith Christ had made them free. "Blessed are the peacemakers, for they shall be called the children of God." St Paul was now one of these; and with rare tact and courtesy he discharged the duty.

The reconciliation of those at variance, is ofttimes a difficult and ungracious task; and in this case it was peculiarly so. Christian as Philemon had become, it was not easy, all at once, to uproot or modify the old, harsh, cruel, contemptuous feelings entertained towards slaves. They were considered as a degraded race and caste, occupying a lower human platform altogether. As we have seen, too, the robbery, or purloining of Onesimus, would naturally not tend to abate these prejudices, or to pave the way to a kindly consideration of his case. In one word, even as a believer, Philemon had good cause to feel strongly the conduct of this menial. And St Paul, it will be observed, in his attempt at conciliation, never for a moment grounds his plea on right or justice; that would have been repudiated. He does not deny, or even palliate the wrong. He concedes it. Moreover, he ventures no further, at first, than asking *forgiveness;* but yet, behind all, he hints by implication at a larger measure of kindness and generosity on the ground of *Christian principle,*—the ground of that new Gospel-equality which sees in every believer a brother, be he bond or free. The Apostle touches the tenderest chord of Philemon's spiritual obligation to himself, as one of the sons he had begotten in the Gospel (ver. 19), "Albeit, I do not say to thee how thou owest unto me even thine own self besides." Then he throws himself on the goodness of his friend (ver. 21), "Having confidence in thy obedience, I wrote to thee, knowing that thou wilt also do more than I say." Right and might could have done nothing in the case; but love and Christian kindness triumph. St Paul speaks not to his *intellect*, but to his *heart;*—not to the old nature, whose hard precept was "an eye for an eye, and a tooth for a tooth," but to the new regenerated being. He speaks to the master as a Christian, and his plunderer is forgiven; he speaks to the master as a Christian, and his slave is free: not only so, but, as we have reason to believe, that slave is soon back again in Rome by the side of his spiritual father, to tell to others the story of a freedom and enfranchisement unknown to the imperial despot who was then sitting enthroned amid the splendours of the Palatine. What an example is the Apostle in this respect! Paul the tentmaker, now Paul the peace-maker. How often by kindly mediation, by word or by letter, could unhappy divisions be averted, and unhappy misunderstandings healed! Many a breach in families, in households, among neighbours and friends, is made and perpetuated, when a soft answer might turn away wrath.

If St Paul be the model of a Christian mediator and pacificator, PHILEMON is the model of a Christian layman, a Christian master, a Christian *man*. His character, from various inspired touches which intersperse the letter, is all that one could wish to see more frequently embodied and exemplified in modern life. If there were more Pauls and more Philemons in the world, the world would be a better and a happier one.

The sacred writers, as has been well remarked, maintain, generally speaking, a studied reserve and reticence in pronouncing eulogies on character. The present letter, however, forms in this respect a singular exception. Let us glance at the portrait and panegyric here drawn of the wealthy and liberal householder of Colosse, and that, too, by one incapable of fulsome or obsequious flattery. First, we have the foundation of all character in the regenerating, sanctifying, and elevating power of the Gospel. Philemon was not a mere loving man, filled with natural goodness and kindliness of heart: these, rather, are the two pillars on which the structure was reared (ver. 5)—" Thy *love* and *faith* which thou hast towards the Lord Jesus "—Faith *in* Christ, and that combined with love *to* Christ.

Farther, that love was *expansive;*—loving Christ, he must love His people; and he adds (ver. 5)— "Toward the Lord Jesus, and *toward all saints.*" This love, moreover, was not a mere sentiment. It had been "manifested;" it was a matter of notoriety. The Apostle tells us it had caused himself great joy and consolation (ver. 7)— "Because the bowels of the saints are refreshed by thee, brother." And to this Faith and Love was added *Prayer.* His two sister graces were strengthened at the incense-altar. There was a long way between Rome and Colosse. The separating distance prevented St Paul listening to the loving words and sympathy of his dear friends there. But there was one sustaining link which bound them: It was the link and the power of Prayer. He was now hopeful (and his hope was not unfounded) of a temporary release, at least, from imprisonment. If he received it, he knew that he would be largely indebted to the intercessions of his loving distant friends, and among these to Philemon (ver. 22)—"I trust that through your prayers I shall be given to you."

And then, in addition to those qualities which are more or less specified in the letter, there are other touches in the picture we are left and authorised to fill in. We see, at once, that St Paul is writing to no impracticable, unreasonable, inaccessible, opinionative man. But to one who is the reverse ;—kind, charitable, just, and generous —willing to be guided in what is right—only requiring the delicate hint to do a kind thing, and it will be done, even though the natural heart can perform it with an effort. A beautiful character this, when we see so much of the reverse,—men stubborn, self-willed, imperious, censorious, malevolent, standing on what is their right, refusing to yield to better thoughts, wiser advisers, more charitable judgments. Philemon, and such as he, whether rich or poor, learned or unlearned, are the pillars of the truth, the living evidences of a living Christianity. It is that, which, as we found in the case of Timothy, more than the most eloquent preaching, commends the truth of God ;—the Epistles of Christ, "known and read of all men." Let us aspire after such features and elements of character,—the faith which "worketh by love and purifieth the heart, and overcometh the world." Christianity is a gigantic system of love—love to God and love to the whole human brotherhood. "Good-will to men" was one note of the triple song of Christ's natal hour, and descriptive of the whole design and tendency of His Gospel. And this love has its thousand tender fibres, its little courtesies, and politenesses, its thoughtful consideration for the feelings of others. " Be pitiful, be courteous." " Be gentle towards all men." That man has many of the first lessons of Christianity yet to learn, who is surly and querulous, peevish and moody; who takes a pleasure in giving utterance to blunt and rude and inconsiderate expressions. Courtesy is a cheap way of showing kindness; it costs little, but it is worth much. Even in turning away a beggar, or refusing him alms, there is a gracious way of doing it. The noblest type of man—the noblest work of God, is the *Christian Gentleman;* and that household is nearest the Christian ideal, where are studied, most minutely, those delicate offices and interchanges of kindliness, which, like golden threads, run through the warp and woof of everyday life. Among these, undoubtedly, as the case of Onesimus suggests, there is kindly consideration for inferiors. Vulgarity is often mated and associated with rudeness and arrogance and superciliousness to those lower in the scale of social life. It is coarse lips that are most apt to frame themselves to utter defamatory, wrongful, insulting words, to those who occupy a humble position in the world's conventional ranks of rich and poor; just as it has been said, "often the unsightliest and least beautiful insects are those which destroy the fairest flowers." Whereas, see the two greatest specimens of Christian gentlemen I can remember in the Bible—*Philemon* and *the Roman Centurion*. See their kindnesses,—the one to his slave, the other to his military servant and subordinate. It is to be feared that in these days, more attention is paid to dogma and formula, than to such beautiful accessories of the Christian life. Both are important in their way; but the one *ought* not, *dare* not, supersede the other; the fringe should be remembered as well as the beautiful garment. "Let this mind be in you, which was also in Christ Jesus." Love Christ first; and if that love is perfect, it must make itself known, by countless manifestations to all around, as well as in our own characters; in mollifying the temper, curbing arrogance, restraining pride, destroying selfishness; in generous consideration for the wishes and wants and weaknesses, even the foibles of others. "Put on, therefore, as the elect of God, holy and beloved, bowels of mercies, kindness, humbleness of mind, meekness, long-suffering; forbearing one another, and forgiving one another, if any man have a quarrel against any: even as Christ forgave you, so also do ye. And, above all these things, put on charity, which is the bond of perfectness. And let the peace of God rule in your hearts" (Col. iii. 12-15).

We have no further light thrown on the future history of Onesimus. We could have wished to know the particulars of his return from Colosse, and the renewal of his Christian intercourse with St Paul; we could have wished to know the con-

verts made among the masses of heathen Rome
by this first "city missionary;" the possibility
of his having shared with Timothy and others
the last hours of their illustrious spiritual father,
and of repaying, in the only way he could, by the
earnest sympathies of a nature that had been
"forgiven much," that debt of love too great for
any earthly recompense. But on all this, the
sacred narrative is silent.* Let us rather, as
the great practical lesson from this interesting
episode in St Paul's Roman life, think of the
transforming power of that Gospel of the grace
of God, in the case of the vilest and most miserable of sinners. After this story of Divine forgiveness, who need despair? That beautiful promise has been realised by an innumerable multitude now in glory, and will be farther fulfilled
and realised, doubtless, in the case of thousands

---

* In the Epistle of Ignatius to the Ephesians, A.D. 107, he
commends Onesimus, their Bishop, for his singular charity. But
it seems doubtful if this overseer of the Church of Ephesus can
be identified with St Paul's convert and fellow-labourer. Other
traditions speak of him as ordained Bishop of Berœa in
Macedonia ; others, of his having suffered martyrdom in Rome.
—*See Smith's* "*Bib. Dic.*," *in loco.*

still—waking up in penitence and tears from their dream of abject hopelessness and despair: —" Though ye have lien among the pots, yet shall ye be as the wings of a dove covered with silver, and her feathers with yellow gold" (Ps. lxviii. 13).

SERMON VI.

St Paul's Special Salutations from the Saints in Cæsar's Household.

"All the Saints salute you, chiefly they that are of Cæsar's household."—Phil. iv. 22.

VI.

(*Preached at the Porta del Popolo, March* 26, 1871.)

PHIL. iv. 22.

"All the Saints salute you, chiefly they that are of Cæsar's household."

LAST Sabbath, in prosecuting the theme of these discourses—the associations of St Paul with the place of our present sojourn—we selected an interesting example from the case of one in the lowest strata of society, who had become a convert of the great Apostle during his residence in ROME. The text of to-day invites our attention to a remarkable counterpart and contrast to this. It discloses to us individuals, who had been welcomed by him as members of the infant Church of this city, not from among the outcast and the poor, but from among those who occupied the highest social position in the proud capital; whether among the Prætorian Guards, or the civil officers and retainers of the Imperial household.*

The words which I have selected as the subject of discourse, are taken from the closing salutation to his beloved family of believers at Philippi. That city was invested with peculiar interest to St Paul. It was the first in Europe where he had preached the Gospel and planted a Christian Church. Twelve years had now rolled by since the memorable morning, when, outside its gates, he had bent his knee by the river side, and mingled his prayers with

---

* Among these, the Roman martyrology mentions Torpes, an officer of high rank in Nero's palace, and afterwards a martyr for the faith. Chrysostom adds the name of Nero's cup-bearer. —See Cave's "*Lives of the Apostles.*" St Paul himself, as we have already observed, among other individuals of note and nobility, mentions Clemens, and Pudens, and Claudia, and the households of Narcissus and Aristobulus. Though not in one sense of "Nero's household," yet among the "not many mighty" who were called, it is interesting to think even of the possibility, according to tradition, of including the name of Nero's cultured tutor, Seneca. There seems, at all events, strong ground for the surmise, that by means of their mutual friend Burrhus, the great Philosopher and the great Apostle held intercourse with one another in the world's capital. Letters, though of doubtful genuineness, still remain, which are said to have passed between them.

those of Lydia and the other lowly worshippers. They were twelve years bright with mercy. Many were the localities where formerly the rites and impurities of Paganism reigned triumphant, which were now studded with Churches of Christ, and could number hundreds who had received the truth as it is in Jesus. But, just in the midst of his usefulness,—when busied gathering his spiritual trophies, the Apostle had been hurried, as we have seen, a prisoner to Rome. The Philippians hear of it. The long-intervening period has not effaced their affectionate remembrance. St Paul languishes in confinement in the world's capital! They must send a messenger to know his state, relieve his necessities, and assure him of continued sympathy—unabated love. Epaphroditus, one of their own pastors, is selected for the embassy. We can imagine the meeting. The Apostle is seated in his hired house when a stranger enters. Brother embraces brother; or rather, the aged father embraces another son in the faith. The object of the visit is told; mutual tears reveal mutual love; the spirit of the captive revives. Day by day, and night by night, that solitary chamber is cheered by the Philippian believer. They mourn, they rejoice, they pray, by turns, over themselves, their flocks, the Churches of their common Lord! But, the time for the return of Epaphroditus has come. Back he must go to the scene of his own labours. Ere he take a reluctant farewell, St Paul must make him the bearer of some messages of love to his distant friends. On the last night they are together, the Apostle dictates his burning words of consolation and gratitude. It is this very Epistle from which our text is taken! We may still further picture the scene, as the little band of converts in Philippi, wait, in anxious expectation, to hear the tidings of their pastor's mission and the exhortations he bears. They have assembled in their own sanctuary; and from one lip after another, question after question is put with eager haste: —" Is he well?"—" How stands his faith?"—" Are his bonds and imprisonment likely soon to terminate?"—" Is he firm as ever in his God?"—" Are we ever to see his face again in the flesh?" The parchment sheet is unfolded; Epaphroditus reads it to the arrested audience: their tears flow; their hearts rejoice. And as he is drawing to a conclusion, it is to them not the least interesting portion of the letter, to hear the loving salutations and benedictions from the family of the Saints scattered in the Roman capital. In the present instance, however, the Apostle evidently has had little time for the lengthened enumeration of names which marks some of his other Epistles. But if there be room and time for no other, there must be *one* exception;—one household must be singled out and mentioned, as warmest in their greetings. And what is that? Is it the home of some lowly spirit, similar to the first convert among themselves, whose heart (opened by the Lord) was gushing forth with the full tide of Christian love to all His people? No; strange selection! The last house in all Rome, or in all Europe, from which they might have expected a kindly word of Christian salutation, is that specially noted. The infamous despot who now swayed the sceptre of the world, was, as we have repeatedly noted, the impersonation of all that was monstrous in iniquity and crime. Amid the thousand edifices within his capital, surely, at least, in these halls of impurity—that palace of riot, there can ascend no prayer, and be found no Christian! What is impossible with man is possible with God. With God all things are possible. In traversing Rome, you may find representatives of every rank and station, who, having enrolled themselves among the family of believers, have gladdened St Paul's lonesome lodging with their visits, and had kindly messages to send to distant Christian friends. But if you would wish to know, who among them all were stanchest in their faith and deepest in their sympathies, you must seek it amid the dependents (it may be courtiers) of *Nero's* Palace. Yes! we may imagine with what strange feelings these assembled Philippians must have listened to the startling assurance, that while " all the Saints " of Rome saluted them, it was " CHIEFLY *they that are of Cæsar's household.*"

From this apparently unimportant clause at

the close of one of St Paul's letters, we may draw, with the Divine aid, many important lessons and reflections. It is to a few of these that I purpose now soliciting your attention.

I. The text illustrates the doctrine of the *Divine sovereignty in election.* The Bible furnishes us with an emphatic commentary on God's dealings with believers: "My thoughts are not your thoughts, neither are your ways My ways, saith the Lord." In regenerating the heart of man, He would show us that from first to last the operation is His: "*Elect of God:*"—that He stands alone in it; that "it is not of him that willeth, nor of him that runneth, but of God who showeth mercy;"—His the prerogative, His the glory. St Paul's confession must be that of every believer, from the hour he is brought to his knees in the prayerful agony of conviction on earth, to the hour he is brought, with the palm of victory in his hand, before the throne—"By the grace of God I am what I am."

It is true, this great Author as well as Finisher

of the faith, puts signal honour on appointed means; and His *general* instrumentalities are the ordinances of His own institution. The Ethiopian treasurer gets comfort and spiritual joy, when he is in the act of seeking God by reading his Bible: Lydia at her prayer-meeting: Nicodemus in his nightly visits of anxious inquiry. But there are times also when He would show that He works how, and when, and where He pleases;—bringing water out of the flinty rock;—and, as we found in the case of Onesimus, from the rudest and most unpromising material, polishing stones for His spiritual temple. Not to dwell on manifold familiar examples, what have we in the text, but another similar and singular illustration of God's sovereign grace, entering the palace gates of ROME, and that, too, in the reign of her most abandoned Emperor, and during the lawlessness of her most licentious court;— "Cæsar's household" furnishing the main pillars in the Christian Church there;—those whose eyes must have been painfully habituated to sights and scenes all adverse to the reception of the truth; yet, while other eyes were closed, and other Roman hearts hardened, God's saving power overcomes every obstacle, and brings many in these regal halls to own a mightier sceptre and more enduring diadem!

How, or where they were converted, we are not informed. Whether it was by the words of St Paul himself, as they gathered around him in his own hired house; or whether those outside the Palace, who had welcomed the glorious message, communicated it to those within, we cannot tell. All we know is, that there *were Saints* there; that the Gospel had been proclaimed; the Spirit had striven; the iron heart of the Roman had been melted; souls were saved. While, then, we believe what was said of the Saviour's ministry is the grand characteristic still, "The common people heard him gladly;" while, as in the case of the converted slave of Colosse, it is "to the *poor* the Gospel is preached," and *by* the poor the Gospel mainly is received; oh! never let us limit the operation of God's grace and mercy, when we read of that grace entering the Palace of Nero; and that, amid the saintly salutations sent by Roman Christians to the Philippian Church, were included "chiefly they that are of Cæsar's household."

II. The text illustrates the doctrine of *the Perseverance of the saints*. The words would lead us to infer, that He who had so marvellously begun the good work, was as marvellously carrying it on; and, in the language the Apostle addressed to the Romans in his great Letter, making these illustrious converts not only conquerors, but "more than conquerors." The depth and tenderness of one Christian affection here specially noted (their love for their distant brethren), would fairly indicate the more than ordinary strength of all the rest. In other words, we are led to conclude, that so far from the graces of their new nature being gradually chilled when brought into unholy contact with the antagonistic influences around them, they grew, in spite of these, with more than ordinary rapidity. Amid the pollutions of that tainted atmosphere; amid the frowns of haughty cour-

tiers, and the scoffs and ridicule of a crowd of
debased and debasing, corrupt and corrupting
sycophants, they maintained their lofty bearing
and carried their consistent cross,—rendering
unto Cæsar the things that were Cæsar's, but
all this subordinate, to rendering unto God the
things that were God's.

If we hold, therefore, that the "calling" of
those of Cæsar's household is a fine attestation of the *sovereignty* of divine grace, there is
perhaps a more remarkable testimony still, in
their case, borne to the power of God's sanctifying, sustaining, and quickening grace; in the
fact, that, despite of all hostile, counteracting
influences, they were able, in the emphatic terms
used by another Apostle, to " add to their faith,
constancy."* It is easy for us, in an age of fashionable profession, to espouse a Gospel-creed, bear
the Christian name, and be carried down the
smooth, unopposing stream; but here, it was
breasting an impetuous torrent. It was the
lamb venturing in the midst of wolves; it was

---

* In our authorised version rendered *virtue* (2 Pet. i. 5).

proclaiming Christ to be King of kings, in the midst of those whose fawning creed was, "We have no king but Cæsar." Cæsar's household! To them the horrors of the Vatican gardens and amphitheatre, and the rush and rage of their lions, could not be unfamiliar. Too well they knew, that for the Emperor's unnatural and barbarous pastime, it was the hated Christians, the guileless and guiltless Nazarenes, who were the selected victims. And yet, bold as these lions were the hearts in his Palace, which had the fear of God and no other fear. The new-born faith they had espoused, which had imparted to their once grovelling souls a strange, mysterious peace (after years, it may be, of unrest and misery, degradation and impurity), was with them no evanescent conviction, obliterated like the sand rippled by the rising tide. They were advancing believers; growing in faith, and love, and holiness: and though clothed in the livery of Cæsar, they were fearless to declare, in a higher sense, "We have no King but Jesus." The very fact of their thus openly sending a message to their brethren at

Philippi, evidenced that they neither wished to conceal their sentiments nor dreaded to avow their creed.

And how was this? How came the Christians in Nero's Palace to have braced themselves with such boldness and spiritual fortitude? How is it that their graces should expand in the very spot, where one would have expected them rather to wither and die?

This leads me to observe :—

III. The text illustrates yet another Scripture doctrine—that *God proportions grace to trial.* " As thy days, so shall thy strength be." The history of all His saints attests this truth. When the storm rages loudest, the everlasting arms are most firmly round about: when the battle is hottest, there is new armour provided and new strength vouchsafed: when the taper burns with a fitful and sickly glow in the tainted atmosphere, more oil is given. On what other supposition can we explain the moral miracle of Daniel's intrepidity in his den; or the Hebrew worthies walking fearless in the burning flames;

or the heroism of the noble army of martyrs chronicled in after ages, at the record of which we stand at times amazed and confounded? They have all one reply—one explanation—"Yet not I; but the grace of God which was with me." Yes! the thorn in the flesh is endured; the dungeon-vault is transformed into a sanctuary of praise; the fire and the faggot fail to draw a tear or extract a groan;—for He is faithful that promised "My grace is sufficient for thee, for My strength is made perfect in weakness." We may cease to wonder, then, at what otherwise would be all marvel and mystery,—how the believers in the Imperial residence of Nero could remain so "strong in faith, giving glory to God:"—"*He giveth more grace.*" And it illustrates God's dealings with His people still. The hour of trial comes, and grace to bear comes along with it. That cutting sorrow or lacerating bereavement, if it had been contemplated beforehand,—the anticipation, the dark possibility—would have utterly crushed. But the blow has come; and when it *does* come, how wondrously supported! The storm-blast has swept down, perchance, the choicest earthly blessings, and left the solitary pilgrim to tread alone life's dreary highway ;—but strength is vouchsafed; the path is trodden; the heart is upheld: "God, our Maker, giveth songs in the night!"

So, in the higher and more difficult spiritual walk. One has become a Christian. It is in a "Cæsar's household;" all around him threatens to damp his spiritual ardour, and mar his fair hopes, and overturn his resolutions. How can he stand out against the cold indifference, and cruel sneer, and open ridicule, and subtle argument? With Jacob he has to say, "All these things are against me." But the God of Jacob interposes: "Fear not, for I am with thee." 'He tempers the wind to the shorn lamb.' "He giveth power to the faint, and to them that have no might He increaseth strength. . . . They that wait upon the Lord shall renew their strength, they shall mount up with wings as eagles." Yes! your Christian graces will rise out of these very trials: this stern discipline will make the hardier pilgrim, the better soldier;

you will be driven from the creature to the Creator ; from the shivered reed to the living Rock. " Cease ye from man," will lead you to the better alternative, " Trust in the Lord for ever !" If, then, you are at any time tempted, from any peculiarity of external circumstance or condition, to doubt the possibility of remaining faithful to your God when all are unfaithful around, think of this subject and this text ; how while St Paul made honourable and memorable mention of *all* the Saints in ROME, it was "CHIEFLY they that were of Cæsar's household."

IV. A fourth reflection we may draw from the text is—*The harmony which subsists among the whole family of believers.* The converts in Cæsar's household, as we have already observed, were, many of them probably, from among the humbler dependents. But we know also,[*] that they numbered some of nobler blood, and more illustrious pedigree. Be this as it may, even a

---

[*] See Introduction, p. 45, *et seq.*

servant in the Palace of the Sovereign of the world! there was enough in the very thought and name to engender a spirit of haughty and supercilious pride, which, in common circumstances, would have scorned at acknowledging friendly relations with poor strangers. But here, we have those in Nero's Palace not hesitating to send a friendly message to the lowly Christians at Philippi—nay, telling St Paul to give assurance, that of all Saints in ROME, they felt most kindly and greeted "chiefly."

How delightful the holy fellowship the Gospel establishes between believer and believer! It does not *level* human distinctions—far from it :—it honours rank and office as ordinances of God. But, in another sense, it does annihilate these; for the exalted Christian recognises the lowliest as a member of the one great family, of which Christ is the living Head. True, this is a fellowship little understood and recognised in degenerate days, when the love, alike of individuals and of Churches, is waxing cold; when that glorious article, " I believe . . . in the communion of saints," has become with many an effete thing, left to slumber a dead dogma in our creeds. But it was a fellowship unmistakably cherished and practically illustrated in the annals of the early Church. In sending now this salutation to the handful of Philippian believers, Nero's Christian Senator was not ashamed to own the converted gaoler there as a brother; the Christian matron remembered humble Lydia as a sister in the faith. In social position they were different; in *spirit*, they were one in Christ Jesus. The electric spark of divine love, struck in the lodging of the Apostle, passes to the Palace of the world's metropolis; thence it traverses through intervening countries to the lanes of Philippi, and circulates and gladdens wherever a Christian Church is planted and a Christian name is known. Nay, it would seem from the text, that so far from the rank of those who send these special greetings detracting from their strength and cordiality, the new principles of this spiritual life, where vigorously planted, lead rather to a triumph over all arbitrary and conventional distinctions,—conquering pride,—

bringing each to see in his brother nothing but a fellow mortal, a dying creature, a companion pilgrim, a joint-heir! The lofty looks of man are abased; and in lowliness of mind, each esteems other better than themselves. We can well imagine, therefore, it was with no feigned lips or spurious humility, that the converts who had just come forth from Cæsar's presence and the splendour of Cæsar's home, when they learned that St Paul was writing to the humble, lowly followers of Jesus at Philippi, should entrust him to send from them special salutations.

But may we not go further still, and add, as the true cause why the salutation of Cæsar's household was the chief, and their love for their distant brethren in Christ strongest, because their love for Christ Himself was strongest? Like the radii of a circle, the nearer believers approach their Lord as their great centre, the nearer they are to one another. Where the stone falls heaviest, the circles in the quiet lake or pool extend the widest. It was so at *Rome*. Love to God fell deepest on hearts in the halls of Cæsar; and the circles of Christian kindness spread from that as a centre. They embraced the brotherhood of Philippi, and if Saints had been there, they would have made their circumference the world! Where the love of Christ is not, or where the pulse of love beats languidly, there is ever the likelihood of distance and estrangement; of individual Christians crossing and recrossing one another in life's path; of Christian Churches entertaining and reciprocating mutual jealousy and distrust. What can cause the sundered elements of religious society to coalesce, but the magnetising influence of that same divine Love attracting all hearts, and welding together all Christian organisations, in a spirit, at least, of unity and co-operation, if incorporation be found undesirable or impossible. These Churches of a now divided Christendom, have been too faithfully likened to the separate pools of water on the rocky beach, each standing apart and alone. *But*, let the Love of their common Lord rise to its paramount place; like a mighty wave, let it sweep over them all in a new spring-tide of

Pentecostal power and blessing;—then would the weary, and apparently unsuccoured cry for brotherhood—uttered in secret by many a desponding heart—find at last its response: then would the Redeemer's Own prayer be gloriously fulfilled—"that they all may be one" (John xvii. 21).

V. A fifth reflection we may draw from the text is—*The sympathy of suffering Saints.* This is another reason why, in offering the friendly and heartfelt salutations of the Roman Church, St Paul adds "*chiefly* they." The power of Christian love may have done much; that of sympathy in suffering did more.

There is nothing that so sacredly binds together Christian with Christian as trial. Those who before had comparatively little intercourse, have lost, at the same time, a beloved child; or hold in common some other similar sad anniversary. It has established between them a new and holy link. Even where distance forbids acquaintance altogether, when the mother, who has had one of her flock taken away, accidentally reads in the obituary of some other heart similarly broken, what outflowings of tender compassion she has for the far-off stranger, which she never felt before, and never *could* have felt, unless she had herself been in the furnace! It was so (though from a different cause) with the Saints in Nero's Palace. They had heard, through Epaphroditus, of the trials experienced by the Philippian believers at the hands of their pagan brethren. The cause was their own. They were themselves bearing this daily cross; and how can they fail to forward the tribute of their heartfelt sympathy to their fellow-sufferers: to salute them as such; and to remind them that the Christian's motto and watchword is the same in all ages and in all ranks, in the palace and in the cottage, in Rome and in Philippi—"All that will live godly in Christ Jesus shall suffer persecution."

Oh, beautiful feature, also, in true Christianity! the pulsations of a living, loving compassion; taking their rise in the heart of Jesus Himself (the Great—the Greatest of sufferers), on whose bosom of love are in-

scribed the words of dear-bought experience—
"I know your sorrows:"—these sending their
sentient thrill throughout the whole mystical
body; so that "if one member suffer, all the
members suffer with it; and if one member
rejoice, all the members rejoice." Are any
among us afflicted? or has the voice of weeping and lamentation been heard in the dwellings
of our poorer brethren? Let us imitate the
example of the Christians at Rome, by delight-
ing to minister to others "the same consolations
wherewith we ourselves have been comforted of
God." May the result of all our trials be like
theirs; to bind us closer to one another in
sympathy, by binding us closer to HIM;—leading us to feel how light our heaviest chastise-
ments are, in comparison with those contained
in the touching challenge—"Was there ever
any sorrow like unto my sorrow?" and to regard these trials in the noble and exalted light
in which St Paul speaks in this very letter;—
Christ *honouring* His people by thus appointing
them to pass through the ordeal of suffering—
"Unto you it is given in the behalf of Christ,

not only to believe, but also to *suffer* for His sake."

VI. Finally, let us learn from the text, *the universal adaptation of Christianity to the family of man, and to every condition of life.* Whatever be the diversity of circumstance or situation, there is no rank in the graduating scale of society, and no position in the varying phases of human relationship, which forbids us to be followers of Jesus. Daniel the prime minister of all Babylon, and Onesimus the runaway slave; David the minstrel king of Judah, and blind Bartimeus on the wayside begging; Anna the prophetess in the Temple, and Lydia the seller of purple; St Paul amid polished philosophers at Athens, St Paul amid rude sailors buffeting a wintry sea; "Paul the aged" and Timothy the child; the household of the Philippian gaoler, and the household of Imperial Cæsar; all, in these diverse paths, can take up their cross and serve their God.

Nay, more; the text would seem to confirm and illustrate a great and important principle, that when God meets His people, and visits them with His grace, He generally does so while they are prosecuting their ordinary engagements. He does not first call them out of the world (as if godliness and secular duties were incompatible), but He reveals Himself to them while faithfully occupying the sphere, whatever it may be, where His providence has placed them; as if to certify, that while diligent in their wonted business, they may at the same time be "fervent in spirit, serving the Lord." Matthew is sitting at his receipt of custom gathering his tribute, he is called *there*. The fishermen of Galilee are mending their nets on Tiberias' shore, they are called *there*. Souls within the precincts of Cæsar's Palace are to be saved, they are saved *there*. Divine sovereign grace finds them occupying their varied posts in the Halls of the Palatine; and they would exhibit on the most difficult scale that was ever tried, how it is possible for the Christian to be *in* the world, and yet not *of* the world; to remain in Cæsar's household, and yet to maintain intact and uncompromised his allegiance to the

Prince of the kings of the earth. This is confessedly indeed a question of great difficulty and delicacy, and on which it becomes us to speak with extreme caution. For, on the other hand, the duty is equally plain and equally imperative, in choosing the different paths of life, carefully to avoid all doubtful or debatable ground. Wherever we know temptation to be,—wherever we dread that our spiritual interests are in risk of being endangered,—the command is distinct, the duty is paramount— "Come out from among them, and be ye separate, and touch not the unclean thing:"—If ye cannot be in Cæsar's household without being partaker in Cæsar's sins, then "come out," that ye be not partakers in his plagues. But, at the same time, our text would seem to tell us, that it is the highest achievement of the Christian, when a man (strong in the grace of God and resolute in the maintenance of principle), can with moral intrepidity bear his religion along with him in the daily walk, where he knows that religion is slighted: and whether it be the Artisan among his scoffing fellow-workmen, or the Servant among irreligious domestics, or the Ruler among ungodly senators, or the Courtier in a dissolute Palace,—to appropriate the high motto of the Christian, which formed the theme of our opening discourse—"I am not ashamed of the Gospel of Christ." If thus enabled, as the Apostle expresses it, "to stand in the evil day, and having done all, to *stand;*"—to stand in the hottest of the battle, faithful to our colours, true to our God;—how great may be the power we wield, whether in the little or the great world of influence; in rebuking that world's atheism and defiant unbelief; its open hostility; its cold indifference; its covert scepticism;—causing it to take knowledge of us that we have been with Jesus, for "*this* is the victory that overcometh the world, even our faith."

Yes! and possible it is. God would seem to put a type in material nature, to tell how the warmth of Christian grace, and the fire of Christian love, can burn and glow in the midst of all that is cold, and cheerless, and repelling. I speak not of the type I saw, but the other day, in the burning mountain which keeps perpetual vigil over the beautiful bay of Naples ; for that very coronal of flame, and the fiery tresses of lava as then seen streaming from its brow, appeared almost in harmony with the glow of sunshine by day, the halo of serene moonlight by night, and the tints of early spring already flushing the wealth of vegetation at its base. But I speak of a different emblem. Strange and startling is the spectacle which arrests the shivering mariner in the northern seas ;—Mount Hecla, with its frigid slopes wreathed with snow and pendant with icicles; and yet, the living fire bursting from its volcano, pouring down in molten streams, melting the ice-bound sides, and the burning torrents reddening the ocean with their glare ! So may the Christian be, like that volcano, in the midst of a cold and frigid mass of worldliness ;—all around, the winter of spiritual desolation and death. But the volcanic fire of grace has been at work ; down pours the lava-stream of burning love, fervid piety, consistent principle ; and at the sight of this glowing believer—a light in a darkened world—many a reckless mariner on that

world's ocean is arrested; sees and owns the
power of vital godliness, believes and lives!
Such was Daniel, amid the chilling and cheerless atmosphere of the court of Babylon. He
might have enjoyed more spiritual tranquillity
by abandoning his presidency, and (joining his
captive countrymen, as they were seated by the
willowed streams), by musing in secret and seclusion over Jerusalem lost, and longing for Jerusalem restored. But duty forbade him to leave
the Courtier's place; he felt that his God might
there be more glorified,—the cause of truth advanced. Nobly was he enabled to fulfil his
high commission, to speak the Divine Word
before kings, and not be moved. The same Almighty arm which supported Daniel in Darius',
as it afterwards did the Saints in Cæsar's household, will support *us*. Let us "be strong and
of a good courage;" and "though troubles rise,
and terrors frown, and days of darkness fall,"
we can do all things through Christ strengthening us. Whatever be our condition or position in the world, our lot is ordered, not *by* us,
but *for* us. Let us not venture to plead some

peculiarity or hardship of our allotment in life, as an apology or extenuation for compromising principle and not following God. But remembering, that, even in Cæsar's household, grace was given and religion maintained ; be it ours to serve Him, whether amid the world's smiles or the world's frowns : in the palace or in the hut : in the mansion of the great or the cottages of the poor; in the hum of the city's busy industry, or in the seclusion of private life ; and we shall find that in our case will be made true the closing benediction which St Paul sent by Epaphroditus to the Philippian Church—" My God will supply all your need, according to his riches in glory by Christ Jesus."

SERMON VII.

St Paul's Prayer in Rome for Onesiphorus.

"THE LORD GIVE MERCY UNTO THE HOUSE OF ONESIPHORUS; FOR HE OFT REFRESHED ME, AND WAS NOT ASHAMED OF MY CHAIN: BUT, WHEN HE WAS IN ROME, HE SOUGHT ME OUT VERY DILIGENTLY, AND FOUND ME. THE LORD GRANT UNTO HIM THAT HE MAY FIND MERCY OF THE LORD IN THAT DAY: and in how many things he ministered unto me at Ephesus, thou knowest very well."—2 TIM. i. 16–18.

"Salute Prisca and Aquila, and the household of ONESIPHORUS."—2 TIM. iv. 19.

VII.

(Preached at the Porta del Popolo, April 2, 1871.)

2 TIM. i. 16–18.

"The Lord give mercy unto the house of Onesiphorus; for he oft refreshed me, and was not ashamed of my chain: but, when he was in Rome, he sought me out very diligently, and found me. The Lord grant unto him that he may find mercy of the Lord in that day."

WE have here another incidental glimpse given us from St Paul's later Roman life. The Christian, whose generous and heroic kindness is in these words so gratefully recorded, has no other mention made of him in sacred story. Like a transient meteor, he shoots athwart the Apostle's evening sky and then vanishes from sight. But this one entry has embalmed his name amid the holy memories of the Apostolic age, and given him a minor indeed, but yet abiding, place, in the Bible constellation of the great and good. So that wheresoever this Gospel shall be preached throughout the whole world, this also that he hath done shall be spoken as a memorial of him.

At the time when St Paul wrote the words of the text, he was undergoing his second imprisonment. During his previous detention, when occupying his own hired house, with no other restriction than having a soldier of Nero's guard to watch him, many of the brethren, waxing confident by his bonds, were "much more bold to speak the word without fear" (Phil. i. 14). Now, however, the case was altered. The indulgence which had tempered the irksomeness of that first captivity was at an end. During the intervening years, the conflagration of the city, caused by the wanton caprice of Nero, had taken place;* and to

---

* On account of the havoc made by this conflagration, which raged for six days and seven nights without intermission, how changed in outward aspect the city must have been, since the time St Paul entered it under guard from Puteoli! Whole streets and masses of buildings, which at that first approach hid from his view the Esquinal hill, were now swept away; and in

avert from himself the odium of the crime, its
guilty perpetrator had laid it to the charge
of the innocent Christians. The audacious
falsehood was only too successful in rousing
the popular indignation against the sect of
which Paul of Tarsus was the acknowledged
leader. We have good reasons to infer, indeed,
that he was arrested at Nicopolis on the charge
of being implicated in the incendiarism, and
sent by the authorities of that city to be tried
at Rome. Treated no longer as an honourable
state prisoner, but as a common criminal, he
was subjected to a strict military custody—
immured probably either in the traditional

---

their stead, close to the present remains of the baths of Titus, the gigantic pile was erected known as "Nero's Golden House." It was adorned with baths, gardens, and a lake: while his own "Colossus"—an enormous statue of himself—rose 120 feet high from the front of the vestibule. It is a significant comment on the transient nature of earthly glory, that in a few brief years, this gorgeous park and palace were, in their turn, completely erased, in order to make way for a still greater architectural wonder, the present *Colosseum*. Its builder (Vespasian) allowed nothing of all the costly magnificence of his predecessor to be recalled, save by retaining on the site of the lake the name of the "colossal" character of the statue which the new building had superseded. *See Lewin*, vol. ii. p. 937.

Mamertine or in some adjoining dungeon.* If
the rigours of his captivity still permitted the
occasional visits of former friends and associates,
the allowance was made only under severe
restrictions, and at the imminent personal risk
of those who were impelled, for love's sake, to
make the venture. Onesiphorus, a Christian of
Ephesus, was probably one of the earliest of
these visitors. He had heard that his father
in the faith pined in a cell in the distant
capital, and, heedless of the dangers involved
in such a pilgrimage, he visits Rome to cheer
the heart of the illustrious prisoner. The latter,
in writing to Timothy a brief time before his
own martyrdom, thus pours forth the language
of a grateful heart,—"The Lord give mercy
unto the house of Onesiphorus; for he oft refreshed me, and was not ashamed of my chain:
But when he was in Rome, he sought me out
very diligently,† and found me. The Lord

---

* See Introduction, p. 72.

† There is much implied in this strong expression of the
Apostle's (σπουδαιότερον ἐζήτησέν). It denotes alike the difficulty
and danger which beset the mission, and the assiduous pains and

grant unto him that he may find mercy of the Lord in that day."

This prayer of the Apostle is a striking and solemn one. Let us, with the divine blessing, seek to gather from it a few of those thoughts and lessons with which it is replete.

I. Learn, as a general truth,—that which also was suggested in the subject of last Sabbath, but which is still more forcibly brought before us here;—*the power and value of human Sympathy*. Who knows it not? What heart has not kindled under its tender offices?—who has not felt how it soothes, and braces, and gladdens? Take that desolate moment, doubtless well-known, in some one of its varied phases, to most who hear me,—when one of the cherished earth-bowers of happiness has been suddenly and unexpectedly bared and blighted; one of the bright stars expunged from life's firmament;—the saddest feature, perhaps, in the

---

perseverance the affectionate disciple displayed in accomplishing it. "Sought me out with extraordinary diligence." So rendered by Alford.

sorrow, being the quenching of that very sympathy of which we speak;—prompting the lines so familiar to bereft hearts, because so true to their deepest yearnings,—

> "Oh for the touch of a vanished hand
> And the sound of a voice that is still!"—

many can recall how the unutterable anguish of that bereavement was assuaged and solaced, by the timely visit (like a messenger from the upper sanctuary), of some beloved and congenial earthly friend, into whose trusted ear the sorrow was unburdened, the secret and sacred heart-ache confided. How even the mute sympathy of look and presence, when words failed in their utterance, helped to dry the tears and staunch the bleeding wounds!

Or, to take a different experience, also not unfamiliar. In those terrible seasons, perhaps the saddest of the human soul, when overtaken by spiritual darkness,—called to grapple with fierce inward temptation, "the aching misery of earnest doubt;"—how many, by the strong hand of Christian sympathy, have been helped up their " Hill Difficulty!" When some thievish

doubts have been robbing them of their peace;
when (like the Prophet of the desert, as his brave
heart in the hour of loneliness failed him, and
in a paroxysm of weakness and despair he lay
down longing to die),—they have felt themelves
driven from their old moorings, and drifting un-
piloted on a midnight sea,—how sustaining and
reassuring, amid the moanings of the blast, were
the accents of human friendship heard uttering
" Peace, be still;" exorcising the foul spirit of
the storm,—rebuking the winds and the waves,
and restoring the great calm! How often has
sickness, in its hours of weariness and depression, or old age in the midst of its infirmities,
been cheered and tranquillised by the loving
hand and loving voice,—the thousand nameless
offices of considerate human affection, sooth-
ing the aching head, and the trembling, fainting
heart! Blessed is every such Barnabas: Blessed
every such "son of consolation:"—the world
has no nobler inmate. In having such, it is
"entertaining Angels unawares."

More than this,—with all reverence we say it,
—did not He, who was the great Ideal of perfect

Humanity, the Lord Jesus Christ Himself, manifest the affinities of His spotless soul with this same holy emotion? Again and again, during His adorable Life on earth, and specially towards its close, we are called to note His yearning for human (yes, *human*) sympathy. What was the Mount of Transfiguration, but a scene of exalted sympathetic communion; representatives, alike from the Church militant and the Church triumphant, gathered to solace and sustain Him in the dread anticipation of His awful trial-hour? As that hour approached, and the shadows were more densely falling, His longings for personal fellowship with His disciples seemed to deepen and intensify also: "With desire have I desired to eat this passover *with you*, before I suffer." In the climax of His woe in Gethsemane, He sought to alleviate its unimagined bitterness by having, close at His side, the sympathy of those earthly friends He deemed most reliable:—" Tarry ye here and watch *with Me.*" While a new ingredient of sorrow was poured into His cup, when the sympathy, on which He might well have calculated as being unfaltering in its constancy, gave way like a brittle reed;—the sheep scattered as the Shepherd was smitten, and the blood-stained warrior of Edom was left to "tread the winepress ALONE" (Isa. lxiii. 3).

St Paul was, in this, as in other respects, endowed with all the nobler and finer feelings of human nature. He opened his magnanimous soul to the same genial influence, as the flower does its closed petals to the sunlight. Every now and then, we discover these longings for congenial and sustaining fellowship. See how he mourns being "left at Athens *alone!*" What a new man he was, when rejoined by Timothy and Silas! How a former visit to the city of Troas was damped and saddened, because an expected fellow-labourer and friend had not been found;—"My spirit had no rest, because I found not Titus my brother." When the brethren came to meet him at Appii Forum, how his soul revived! He "thanked God and took courage." If he felt thus dependent on human support, even in the hour of manly vigour; how genial and gladdening must such sympathy have been to him at this period of his history, when that buoyancy and gladness, we have previously noted as characterising the period of his first imprisonment, must necessarily, from various causes, have undergone diminution. His energies could not possibly have been what they once were, now that threescore winters were whitening his locks and furrowing his brow; and the lonely exile was left to encounter the privations of a dungeon home. Others in his case, too, as with his Lord before him, had grown faithless. A Demas-throng—his "summer friends,"—smiling on him in his prosperity, when his missionary bark was sailing over summer-seas—borne on with propitious breezes—had turned cowards in his adversity. One after another, they had left the sinking ship to its fate, as the storm-clouds were gathering! Not, however, all. A few tried and trusted ones (and Onesiphorus among them), had planted themselves by the side of the venerable Pilot as he resigned himself to a hero's death, and were willing, if need be, to go down with him in the waters. As the ivy clings kindliest around the old, furrowed, battered ruin, so St Paul could discover who his true friends were, when he had become such an one as 'Paul the aged.' Onesiphorus brought him no offerings that we know of. But the tear in his eye, the kind word, the warm grasp of his hand, were like cold water to that thirsty soul. We may think of the two in this Roman prison: what deathless ties, sympathetic cords, linked them to one another! What glorious themes warmed their hearts, tuned their lips, and evoked their prayers and praises! Their Master's name, His cause, His kingdom, His matchless love, His upholding grace, His coming glory, the Church on earth, the Church in heaven! Their own common trials, perplexities, solaces, hopes! When Onesiphorus came to leave ROME for Ephesus, the remembrance of his visit lingered in the Apostle's heart, like the music of home voices in the midnight sea. The unbefriended prisoner dwells on it, as a bright spot in his captivity. And as he now writes a letter to his best beloved Timothy, asking from him a similar boon—that he would hasten to see him before he dies,—he cannot resist telling, in a parenthesis, of this ray of kindness that had shot across his darkened sky; how that, while all they of Asia had turned from him, one of the citizens of its great capital had proved a noble exception, for he had "*oft refreshed him, and was not ashamed of his chain.*"

II. Let us note, as a second lesson, *the sublime recompense of Prayer*. St Paul could not in any wise remunerate his friend. Silver and gold he had none. Even if such had been a befitting acknowledgment, he possessed it not. What had *he* to give, who was himself so destitute of needful comforts, as to write Timothy in Asia Minor—as we specially noted when speaking of that strongest and fondest of his friendships—to bring with him the old cloak he had left at Troas, that it might aid to shelter his aged frame from the chill damps of his dungeon? But *one* recompense he has. Yes; he can restore Onesiphorus a hundredfold. He can carry his case to the great Recompenser. He can plead God's own promised benediction—"Blessed is he that considereth the poor, the Lord shall deliver him in the time of trouble." As we found in the case of St Paul and Philemon regarding Rome and Colosse; so was it also with Rome and Ephesus. These were geographically far distant. The Great Sea lay between them. But a wire and electric fluid, more wondrous than science and ocean in our day have dreamt of, united the two. It connected together the two cities on earth, and both with the Throne of God. The memory of his friend's sympathising visit flits before the eye of the Apostle; and as he is narrating the fact to his son in the faith, he must interrupt for a moment the thread of his Epistle, to breathe a passing prayer—" The Lord give mercy to the house of Onesiphorus. The Lord grant that he may find mercy of the Lord on that day." That prayer, doubtless, ascended not unanswered. There would be blessings innumerable, though we are told not of them, which fell on the distant household.

It is striking to observe that it is "the *house* of Onesiphorus" (not Onesiphorus personally), for which the prayer is offered. The question naturally occurs, What are we to understand from this? It may be, that no more is intended but that the Apostle's large heart would embrace the whole household of his friend; that as the house of Obededom was blessed on account of the Ark, or as the family of Saul were dealt with kindly for Jonathan's sake, so does he pray, regarding small and great in that distant Ephesus home, that God would surely bless them! But we may assign to it, as some commentators have done, a different interpretation. The name of Onesiphorus is mentioned by St Paul once more, in the close of this Epistle. It is mentioned among the salutations to *individual friends*. But again, as here, it is "the *household* of Onesiphorus" of which he makes mention, not of himself: "Greet Aquila and Priscilla and the *household* of Onesiphorus." Does not this give a strong probability to the surmise, that that self-denying disciple, so lately ministering to a suffering member of the Church below, had, when the Apostle wrote, been admitted a glorified member of the Church above? In other words, that he had predeceased his be-

loved spiritual Father—won before him the
martyr's crown. It gives an affecting interest
and beauty to this touching Bible incident. St
Paul's kind visitor was beyond the need and
reach of his prayers. But the sepulchre had not
closed over the memories of that visit. The
dark tomb or the martyr's axe had not cancelled
the obligations of Christian gratitude. If the
grass of Ephesus be waving over his friend's
grave, or if his martyr-ashes have been strewn
in insult on the waters, he can claim for
the orphaned "household" the blessing of the
Father of the fatherless. Long after the
Apostle's own dust was laid in its resting-place,
that dungeon-prayer, uttered from a full heart,
may have proved to *one* home in Ephesus, amid
the whirlwind of persecution (as the scarlet
thread of Rahab at Jericho), an unknown
spiritual heirloom,—entailing mysterious blessings (temporal and spiritual) upon children's
children.

Be this as it may; here, at all events, is a
recompense which every one can bestow; the
noblest and best of all returns for earthly kind-

ness. You can give this, when you can give no other—*the recompense of prayer*. Ay! and prayer, too, can fetch down blessings on the absent: it annihilates space; it knows nothing of distance. That friend, that brother, the companion of your youth, is far separated from you,—out on the perilous ocean, away in the distant colony. The sound of the Sabbath-bell falls no more on his ear; you can go with him no longer to the house of God in company; his place is vacant in the pew; his chair is empty at the table; his voice is missed at the home-hearth! But you *can* be present with him. Prayer can bring you to his side. Prayer can whisper a father's blessing over him. Prayer can sprinkle him with better than a mother's tears. Prayer can fetch the angels of God around him as a guard; his shield in danger, his defence in trouble. Far off in her cottage-home, a thousand miles away, a mother, all unconscious at the moment of the danger of her sailor-boy, is uttering her midnight intercession for the wanderer. It has ascended at the very crisis of destruction. The cry of the trembling form kneeling by her lonely couch has rocked the waves to rest. It is a mother's "effectual fervent prayers" that have turned the storm into a calm!

Prayer is still the golden key by which we can unlock for others as well as for ourselves the treasury of Heaven and "move the arm of Omnipotence." What we owe, on the other hand, to the prayers which have hovered over our cradles, followed us into the world, grappling for us in our strong temptations, and which, like Jacob wrestling with the Angel, have prevailed, will never be known until that Day when the secrets of all hearts shall be revealed!

III. Observe next, *the special boon desired*. It is *Mercy*. "The Lord give *mercy*." "The Lord grant that he may find *mercy* of the Lord." Mercy is a sinner's word. It is the pity which God shows to the undeserving. *Goodness* is the term we use when we speak of His kindness as displayed to His unsinning creatures; mercy is His kindness in its manifestation to the miserable and lost. When our souls were lying like stranded vessels on the beach, the tide of this ocean-mercy set them again floating on the waters. Mercy is the highest type and expression of the divine Goodness. In Heaven, the ascription of the unredeemed angels is—"God is Love." When they think of their own rebel hosts and the penalty of apostasy, their cry is—"God is Holy." When they think of redeemed man, it is—"The Lord, the Lord God, *merciful* and gracious." Mercy is the offended Sovereign proclaiming amnesty to rebels—lifting the beggar from the dunghill, and setting him among princes. *Mercy*—"the mercy of God." It is a brief sentence. It can be lisped by a child; but what seraph can fathom the depths of its meaning? An inspired Apostle, baffled in the attempt, seems only able to shadow forth its wonders by thus heaping together superlatives: "God, who is rich in mercy, for His great love wherewith He loved us, even when we were dead in sins" (Eph. ii. 4, 5). Amazing thought! God's mercy stooping over us, and His love loving us, when we were morally and spiritually *dead*. Did you ever hear of one loving the dead?

'Yes!' a hundred lips reply; 'we *have* loved the dead! We have wept and sobbed over the cold marble;—we have loved to gaze on those rayless eyes, although the light of life has faded from them for ever here;—with an unutterably sacred affection have we loved the broken, mutilated casket, even when the bright jewel had departed.' But this is not the case in point, in estimating the marvels of the mercy of God. Let us ask rather—Did you ever love the dead outcast on the street? Did you ever love the beggar found, wrapped in rags for his shroud, lying on the open highway? No! though you may have pitied him, compassionated him; though you may have shuddered at the spectacle—no tear of *love* could bedew your cheek. But if human compassion is unable to tell so wondrous a tale, "Let the *redeemed* of the Lord say so, whom He hath redeemed out of the hand of the enemy." God has done this. God's mercy has reached the point of loving the dead outcast—ay! more—loving the dead enemy: "*Even when we were dead in sins!*" That mercy of God in Christ embraces, too, the vilest and most miserable. None stand beyond its pale. No gate—no veil—no flaming sword of cherubim bar the way to the mercy-seat. Our sins may have reached unto the clouds, but the heights of the divine mercy are loftier still: "As the heavens are high above the earth, so great is His *mercy* towards them that fear Him." Appropriately surely the inspired comment and exhortation seems to follow—" Let us, therefore, come boldly unto the throne of grace, that we may obtain *mercy*."

It is this "mercy of the Lord" which St Paul here invokes for his sympathising visitor. There is something, perhaps, at first sight, strange in the Apostle's prayer in relation to him who was the object of it. It is not what we would have looked for in the circumstances. Onesiphorus had come on an errand of self-denying love—a noble episode in that age of spiritual heroism. When the Apostle prays for him, we almost look for some such petition as this—'The Lord reward him for his deeds! Lord! there is much that this man hath done for me. Great has been his faith, his devotion, his unselfishness, his considerate sympathy to me, Thy prisoner. He has braved perils of the sea, and perils of the city, and perils of false brethren, in order to cheer me in my hour of loneliness and sorrow. Let not the cup of cold water given to Thy disciple, go without the promised blessing. Recompense his kindness according to its deserts. Let it be returned a thousandfold into his own bosom!' No! he remembers him only as a *sinner:* "The Lord have *mercy* on him!"

St Paul would remind us here, of the one only ground of hope and confidence and trust we have in the sight of a holy God. He was indeed the last to undervalue the precious fruits of the Spirit, as manifested in the heart and the life of the true believer. In the soul that has been divinely sanctified and purified, there is much to love and admire;—those Christian graces—holy affections and holy deeds—flowers in the Beloved's garden, which, like so many incense-censers, are sending up their fragrant perfume to heaven. These, doubtless, are regarded with divine complacency now; and at the Great Day, they will draw from the lips of the Righteous Judge the divine approval and encomium—"Well done, good and faithful servant!" But what would all these (the best of them) avail, when we come to regard them as forming the sinner's plea at that bar of unswerving rectitude and equity? A poor instalment, verily, in the discharge of an infinite debt. To use the words of a writer, it would be "an attempt to pay off that debt at one end by pence, which has been accumulating by talents at the other." If the Apostle himself once indulged some such dreams of personal merit and sufficiency, the further he advanced in the divine life,—the more maturely he grew in grace and holiness and purity; in a word, the nearer he approached to God, the more deeply did he feel his need of *mercy*. Hear the estimate he gives of his own character and spiritual worthiness, and that too not in his earlier, but in his closing and riper years:—"Less than the least of all saints;"—"Sinners, of whom I am the chief." In writing to Timothy from Rome, the most joyful word he can utter when he thinks of himself, as "before a blasphemer and persecutor and injurious," is this—"*But* I obtained MERCY." It is the same boon he seeks for Onesiphorus, to which he clings, as his own—his only, unfailing anchorage. Yes! come and learn from this giant in grace, when standing on the borders of the grave, the alone foundation of a sinner's, or rather a believer's hope. With all the memories of his apostleship behind him, a thousand battles of the faith, in which, as a spiritual champion, he had fought and bled and conquered: with the remembrance of Jewish hate and Gentile scorn; the stocks and stripes of Philippi; the buffeting of winter tempests he had braved by land and sea; the moral intrepidity that made him stand amid Athenian philosophers, in the streets of Imperial Rome, and amid the merchant princes of Corinth, pleading the injured cause of his Great Master; the sacrifice of home, country, friends, religion, for a life of untiring and perpetual exile from most of the world's amenities and joys,—like a weary bird having no rest for the sole of his foot, and seeking none; and now with the flash of the executioner's sword before him, to close the mighty drama of a consecrated existence: Yet hear his final plea, —" I *obtained* MERCY ;" hear his final prayer,— it is *mercy* for himself, *mercy* for his friend— " The Lord grant unto him that he may find mercy of the Lord in that day!" Could we follow St Paul and Onesiphorus now, among yonder bright martyr-multitude before the throne, we might listen to their joint-song. The dungeon-prayer has been caught up in Paradise: it is the song of Eternity—" O give thanks unto the Lord, for He is good, for His *mercy* endureth for ever!"

IV. Once more, let us observe *the Great Day of recompense*, on which the Apostle's thoughts and prayers are centred: " The Lord grant unto him that he may find mercy of the Lord *in that day.*" " *That* day." We look for some antecedent in the verse, or in some preceding one. We can find none. How is this? Ah! it is beautifully significant. It tells us of some time—some era in this illustrious man's mind—which outpeered, in solemn importance and interest, all others; some vast epoch with which he was so familiar, that unconsciously, in writing to another, he does not name it. Timothy would need no interpreter as he read his letter. It was *the Great Day of God;* that luminous, radiant day, when Christ would appear in the glory of His Father and of the holy angels, as the Judge both of quick and dead.

This is not the only passage where St Paul makes a similar indirect reference to the Day of final reckoning. In the 12th verse, which we shall afterwards more specially consider, he says, "I know whom I have believed, and am persuaded that He is able to keep that which I have committed unto Him against *that day*." Again, in the 4th chapter and 8th verse (it is striking, these occurring in his last letter, as if the Great white Throne were in view), "Henceforth there is laid up for me a crown of righteousness, which the Lord, the righteous Judge, shall give me at *that day*." It was a glorious beacon-light in the haven of Eternity, which had gladdened his spirit during many a midnight on earth's tempestuous sea; but it was shining clearer and brighter as he was nearing the heavenly shore.

Need we wonder that he and the members of the suffering, struggling Church in that early age, regarded the Advent of Christ on His Throne of Judgment, as their most "blessed hope," and made it the object of their constant and longing prayers? that it was looked forward to as the birthday of the Church-triumphant; the day when the wrongs of earth would be righted; when sin would be expelled, and Satan bound; when their living, loving Lord would be crowned with many crowns; "the day of His espousals; the day of the gladness of His heart." To St Paul it had other peculiar features of attractiveness. It was the true antitype of the "Feast of Ingathering"—the harvest-home of Heaven; the day on which many, like him, who had gone forth "weeping, bearing precious seed," would come again with rejoicing, bringing their sheaves with them. Was it strange, that the day uppermost in his thoughts—the day of days,—that which was so familiar in his forecast of the future, that he need give it no other distinctive appellation—was the one which would not only permit him thus to witness the public coronation and enthronement of his Redeemer before an assembled world, as Lord of all, but which would usher him also into the presence of the Saints he had been honoured to save. "Without fault before the throne" they would "that day" stand, clothed in the full and final glory of their resurrection bodies. "What," says he, "is our hope, or joy, or crown of rejoicing? Are not even ye in the presence of our Lord Jesus Christ at His coming" (1 Thes. ii. 19).

That day!—The chained, lonely captive in his gloomy ward, with the tear of gratitude in his eye, could picture Onesiphorus among the crowd who are then represented as thus disavowing the good deeds with which the Great Judge had credited them: "When saw we thee in prison, and came unto thee?" He could listen in thought, to the gracious reply, identifying him with his friend, and making a blissful memory of earth, a memory of heaven, "Inasmuch as ye have done it unto one of the least of these My brethren, ye have done it unto Me."

To what can we urge all here present, in preparation for that day and its solemn verities, but to seek that *mercy*, that same rich *mercy* which St Paul sought for Onesiphorus ; to take the publican's place, and, with the tear of penitence in your eye, and the prayer for pardon on your lips (looking too, as he did, to the Altar of Sacrifice,*) to utter the cry of the broken spirit, " God be *merciful* to me, a sinner !" We believe there is no bound or barrier to that ocean of mercy in Christ, save what is erected by the pride, or indifference, or unbelief of man. It laves and washes the rockiest shores of the rockiest heart. St Paul tells us for our encouragement, why that rich mercy was exercised towards him. " Howbeit for this cause I obtained *mercy*, that in me, first " (*first*, not in point of time, but in point of guilt), " Jesus Christ might show forth all long-suffering, for a pattern to them which should hereafter believe on Him to

---

* Ἱλάσθητι, implying reconciliation through sacrifice.

life everlasting" (1 Tim. i. 16). But remember, it must be mercy *sought now*, to be mercy *found* on that day. We can pray for you now, as St Paul did for his friend; you can pray for yourselves; but "that day" once come, Omnipotence itself cannot undo a neglected past!

Nor let any venture to trust in the vain delusion, that the mercy to be extended then, is the exercise of God's sovereign attribute; that He will be too kind and too gracious to deal out the full measure of His threatenings; that He will relax the severity of His law; that He will suffer "them that fell" to taste only His "goodness," not His "severity."—Say, would the cross of Calvary have been erected; would His own dear Son have had poured upon Him the vials of redundant suffering and anguish, if, after all (independent of these sufferings), Mercy could thus finally triumph over Justice? No! God is "not a man that He should lie, neither the son of man, that He should repent." While His mercy is from everlasting to everlasting on them that fear Him, it is a mercy founded on everlasting Truth and everlasting

Righteousness. God too merciful to punish! That august tribunal will overturn this, along with every other false confidence. Those who cling to the illusion will find it a rope of sand in riding out the final storm.

Oh! when that momentous crisis-hour shall come, when the Lord shall arise in the glory of His majesty, the centre and focus of a congregated world; when that Throne shall be set, before whose sapphire brightness sun and moon will grow pale; when the whirlwind of His wrath will be sweeping down every refuge of lies; when the heavens shall be folded together as a scroll,—passing away with a noise, compared with which the loudest thunder would be but as an infant's cry; when the earth shall be the sport of devouring flames, its forests charred into blackness, and its hills become as chaff; when the graves of centuries shall be rifled, and the tramp shall be heard of gathering millions marching to the Great Assize — The Lord grant unto us, that we may find mercy of the Lord on THAT DAY!

SERMON VIII.

St Paul's Dying Testimony in Rome. His Martyrdom. Conclusion.

"For the which cause I also suffer these things: nevertheless I am not ashamed; for I KNOW WHOM I HAVE BELIEVED, AND AM PERSUADED THAT HE IS ABLE TO KEEP THAT WHICH I HAVE COMMITTED UNTO HIM AGAINST THAT DAY."—2 TIM. I. 12.

"For I am now ready to be offered, and the time of my departure is at hand. I have fought a good fight, I have finished my course, I have kept the faith: henceforth there is laid up for me a crown of righteousness, which the Lord, the righteous Judge, shall give me at that day; and not to me only, but unto all them also that love His appearing."—2 TIM. IV. 6-8.

VIII.

(Preached at the Porta del Popolo, April 9, 1871.)

2 TIM. i. 12.

"I know whom I have believed, and am persuaded that He is able to keep that which I have committed unto Him against that day."

WITH what more appropriate theme than this, could I conclude the series of subjects which have engaged our attention during my brief ministry in this city? These touching words of St Paul have a sacred solemnity attached to them, far exceeding that which belongs in common to all dying utterances. If, as children, we gather in rapt reverential emotion around the couch of a departing parent, and treasure up the sayings of the hour in everlasting remembrance (all the more so, if that parent's teachings and counsels have formed our unerring guide through life), with what hallowed interest should we, as Christians, gather around the closing hours of one, who, next to the Divine Redeemer he served, was the wisest, greatest, most loving of men; and watch, so to speak, the last throbs of that mighty heart which "stirred the pulses of the world?"

The verse itself, as you already well know, forms part of the final letter the great Apostle dictated. He had now successfully rebutted the first indictment brought against him at Nero's tribunal; that which, in all probability, consisted of the charge of complicity with incendiaries in the burning of Rome. Even the debased Emperor himself, if he gave a personal hearing to the case, was apparently unable to resist the weight of evidence establishing the prisoner's innocence. According to St Paul's own words he was "delivered out of the mouth of the lion." He was remanded to gaol, to wait the second and final stage of his trial, in which the more important accusation was to be dealt with, of being the leader of a sect whose doctrines were in direct hostility to the national faith, involving treason against the Emperor. Too well did he know, that this major 'count' could not,—dared not,—be repelled like the former; and with that calm heroism, which never forsook him in all the trying exigencies of the past, he prepared for the worst. As we have previously noted, he was left, too, at this eventful crisis, well-nigh alone; condemned to mourn in secret and solitude over the dereliction of former associates and friends. Some of these, indeed, at great personal risk, still cheered with an occasional visit the gloom and loneliness of his prison. Others, linked to him in fervid and unabated affection, had all the will openly to avow their attachment and prolong their services, but they were deterred by the almost certain vengeance that would have overtaken them. They would not only have been branded for connivance with the chief of an illicit religion, but they would have shared the odium he had incurred, from the thousands who had been rendered houseless and homeless, in consequence of the crime maliciously laid to his charge. So great was the terror inspired by this first "imperial persecution" against the Christians, that when the Apostle had lately stood in the Basilica of the Palatine, confronted by his judges, he tells us he found himself entirely unsupported. No advocate could be secured to help him in his defence; no companion to cheer him with his sympathy, or to be identified with his cause. "At my first answer," says he, "no man stood with me, but all men forsook me." While such was the position, reluctantly assumed, by not a few of those who were still devoted to himself, and still loyal to his Great Master, there were others who had turned basely renegade. From his paternal adjuration to Timothy, "Be thou not *ashamed*," and by his complimentary reference to Onesiphorus, "He was not *ashamed* of my chain," we gather, by implication, that there were others who were;— others who had quailed before the coming storm, and abandoned the noble vessel to wrestle, as best it could, among the breakers. Craven-hearted themselves, they had apparently tried to appeal. to the old prisoner's fears. Now that he had been acquitted on the minor indictment, might he not be prevailed upon to evade the certain consequences of the second, by renouncing at once the hated creed, and doing homage to Cæsar? Nothing else, nothing less, could save him. Nero had re-enacted, in their full vigour, the intolerant laws which had been repealed by Claudius, and which imperatively required from all an acknowledgment of the reigning Emperor as divine;—demanding the offering of sacrifices in his name, and his being addressed by the title of 'Lord.' As St Paul possessed the privilege of "citizenship," he might on that account the more readily, by a timely recantation, have had his past offences against the State condoned, and have saved himself from condign punishment. When these unworthy advisers, of whom I have spoken, saw the giant power of Rome arrayed against the infant faith; —that faith itself, apparently, a mere 'bubble among the breakers,'—a brittle reed, with no human possibility of surviving the persecution which had burst upon it in demon fury: might they not be supposed thus to argue with him, in the moment of their own weakness and apostasy—'Why, Paul, persist in the hopeless cause, and prolong the hopeless conflict? Why maintain an unequal struggle for that, which, being in antagonism to the Empire's belief, and to the will of the Cæsars, must, sooner or later, fall to the ground? Why perish in the flames or by the sword, for what is doomed to perish with you?' 'Nay,' would be his reply; 'disturb me not. Clinging to that faith in which I have lived, and for which I am now ready to die, is no act of wilful, blind fanaticism,—the reckless devotion of a visionary dreamer, to a doomed and desperate cause. I have nobler and loftier anticipations regarding that for which I suffer. I have a grander confidence in the majesty of truth, than to suppose that it can eventually be crushed and overthrown by the base tyranny and hostility of man. I have appealed to a more righteous bar. That God, who sent His Angel to me in the midst of the storm, will not leave me now. He has delivered me, and He will yet deliver me from the lions' mouth. My enemies may do their worst. They may insult my gray hairs; they may load me with irons; they may doom me to the public exposure of the circus; they may burn my poor body and scatter its ashes on that Tiber; but, "nevertheless I am not ashamed: for I know whom I have believed, and am persuaded that He is able to keep that which I have committed unto Him against that day."'

Such seems to be the import of these glowing words. May the Apostle's creed be ours, ours his triumphant faith, that ours at last may be his eternal reward!

We have three topics here suggested for consideration :—

    I. A joyful assurance regarding the present.

    II. A happy persuasion regarding the future.

    III. The glorious prospect of a Day of final triumph.

I. We have *a joyful assurance regarding the Present.* "*I know whom I have believed.*" The first thing which strikes us in this assertion is its wording. The *formula* is remarkable. The Apostle does not say, 'I know *what* I have believed,' but "I know *whom* I have believed;" or (as that is better rendered in the margin), "I know whom I have *trusted.*" It is not facts, or doctrines, or confessions, or sects, or Churches he speaks of, but his *Living Lord* :—" It is not even Christianity he boasts of, but Christ." " Detach Christianity," it has been beautifully said, " from Christ, and it vanishes before your eyes into intellectual vapour. For, it is of the essence of Christianity, that day by day, hour by hour, the Christian should live in conscious, felt, sustained relationship to the ever living Author of his creed and life. Christianity is non-existent apart from Christ; it centres in Christ; it radiates now, as at the first, from Christ. It is not a mere doctrine bequeathed by Him to a world with which He has ceased to have dealings, it perishes outright, when men attempt to abstract it from the living Person of its Founder."[*] St Paul felt so ; and this dying confession of his faith, is quite what we would have expected from him. The motto of his existence was this—" To me to live is Christ,"—" Christ my life." Life to him was a hallowed journey with Jesus at his side. He loved Him, and leant upon Him as

---

[*] Liddon's Bampton Lectures, 1866, p. 192.

an earthly friend; like the sunflower opening to
the radiant beams, and drooping in sadness and
sorrow when that sun is away. Belief, too, was
with him, not a mere mental act—the cold calcu-
lating subscription of reason. It was the cleav-
ing, trustful homage of a devoted heart; a loyal
allegiance of the intellect, the thoughts, the
motives, the will, the affections, to the Redeemer, as absolute Lord and ever-present
King. Neither parent, nor sister, nor associate
in his old Tarsus home, did he ever love like
this Jesus of Nazareth. He had tried Him, and
he had never found Him to fail. He therefore
rejects with scorn the appeals of his timid and
treacherous advisers, to purchase immunity from
suffering by a base denial of his Lord. That
trust of his was no enthusiastic dream. He had
not abandoned home or kindred; he had not
forfeited all he loved and valued on earth for
the bauble of an hour. He had counted the
cost: he had tested this "Stone laid in Zion;" he
had found Him "a tried stone, a sure foundation." The heights above might combine with
the depths beneath; fiendish men might be con-

federate with fiendish devils, in trying to shatter his confidence, and blight his hope; but none would be able to separate him from the love of God which is in Christ Jesus his Lord!

> " When Persecution's torrent blaze
> Wraps the unshrinking martyr's head :
> When fade all earthly flowers and bays,
> When summer friends are gone and fled ;
> Is he *alone*, in that dark hour,
> Who owns the Lord of love and power?
>
> " Or, waves there not around his brow
> A wand no human arm can wield,
> Fraught with a spell no angels know,
> His steps to guide, his soul to shield ? "

"Alone! yet not alone"—"The Captain of the Lord's host" was with him—"The LORD," he says, "stood with me and strengthened me." It was not in vain that he was then consummating the life-long act of 'pouring out' his consecrated existence as a libation on God's altar.* The Great Angel of the Covenant was there, to accept the offerer and the sacrifice. Perfumed

---

* Such is the literal meaning and reference in the words, "I am now ready to be offered" (σπένδομαι),—"poured out as a drink-offering," used only in one other passage in St Paul's Epistles, Phil. ii. 17.

with other merits than his, the incense-cloud went up with acceptance before God.

And what are the grounds of this confidence in the case of every believer, as well as in that of St Paul? It is trust in a *living* Saviour, grounded on the meritorious obedience and sufferings of a *dying* Saviour. As we saw, in last Sabbath's discourse, there was a time when this great Champion of the faith would have trusted in anything rather than this. There was a time when he would have "trusted in himself that he was righteous, and despised others." "I was alive," was the boaster's challenge, "without the law once"—'I thought all was well with me; that I was in a fair way for Heaven; I soared in my religious profession high above my fellows. *But*, "when the commandment came;"—when the abysmal deeps of my own defilement and depravity yawned beneath me, and the exceeding breadth of God's law was disclosed to my illuminated vision, "sin revived, and I died." I who once fancied myself a living man, pronounced myself spiritually dead!' Surely, if ever the child of Adam could enter Heaven on the ground of his own doings, it was he who penned our text;—whose life-motto was this, "*always abounding* in the work of the Lord." Think of his graces as a Christian, his success as a minister, his labours as an Apostle. Who more than he had *earned* his crown? who more than he could take his stand at the bar of God loaded with merit? How different! As we described more fully on a previous occasion, all his own once boasted righteousness is like the yielding ice beneath his feet. It melted before the blaze of God's throne of purity. In the present hour of approaching dissolution, just when this mighty Tree in God's forest seemed (like the birchen trees we have all seen in our own land in their golden autumn tints) grandest in decay; just as his soul is about to wing its eagle-flight to the spirit-world, "Christ and Him crucified" is clung to with an ever fonder, holier trust.—"This is a faithful saying, and worthy of all acceptation, that Jesus Christ came into the world to save sinners!"

Have *we* the same blessed assurance and joy in contemplating the Work and Person of

Jesus? Lost, and perishing, and undone by nature, have we been able to cast ourselves, from first to last, on the merits and righteousness of our Surety-Redeemer? Have we seen in Him, the true "Rainbow of Emerald," proclaiming in its blended tints and sublime harmonies, that while "justice and judgment" are the habitation of God's throne, "mercy and truth" may go continually before His face; for in the doing and dying of Christ the lustre of a sublime vindication encircles every attribute of His nature, and every requirement of His law? And exulting in the completed atonement of Jesus, can we share, in some feeble measure, the Apostle's joy in contemplating a personal, living, loving Saviour? Christ in our nature; susceptible of every human sympathy; bending over us with His pitying eye; entering with infinite tenderness into every human want and woe; drawing nigh in all the dark experiences of life, as He did to the disciples on their midnight sea, and whispering the calming words, "It is I," (or rather, "I AM"), "be not afraid." 'I am the Living One; I am the controlling One (aye, and to "as many as I love"); I am the rebuking One, and the chastening One!' Let us think of this, not as a cold abstraction, or beautiful phantasm, but as a glorious truth, a sublime and comforting verity. He is ever with us! When the gates of the morning are opened; swifter than the arrowy light, His footstep of love is at our threshold. When the gates of the evening revolve on their silent hinges, and day merges and melts into twilight, He is there! Amid the bustle of life, in "the loud stunning tide of human care," He is there! By the lonely sickbed, when the glow of health has left our cheek, and the dim night-lamp casts its flickering gleam on our pillow, He is there! When the King of terrors has entered our dwellings;— when we are seated amid the awful stillness of the death-chamber, listening in vain for the music of cherished voices, hushed for the forever of time, He is there! In all these diverse experiences, He draws near in touching tenderness, saying, "Fear not, I am He that liveth and was dead; and behold I am alive for evermore." "Fear not: for I have redeemed thee;

I have called thee by thy name; thou art mine. When thou passest through the waters, I will be with thee; and through the rivers, they shall not overflow thee: when thou walkest through the fire, thou shalt not be burnt; neither shall the flame kindle upon thee. For I am the Lord thy God, the Holy One of Israel, thy Saviour."

II. Let us proceed, as we purposed, to consider *the Apostle's happy persuasion regarding the future.*—"*I am persuaded that He is able to keep that which I have committed unto Him.*" St Paul exults in Christ's sufficiency in the past; He rejoices in Christ's love in the present; and now, the future, with all its unrevealed secrets, he commits to the keeping of that same Saviour God. "He is able to *keep.*" Blessed name, blessed title! Christ the Keeper of His people; their Shelter, their Citadel, their Stronghold; where He *keeps* them "in perfect peace." He, the heavenly Casket, holding in sacred custody all they confide to Him;—they, committing their souls to Him in well-doing;—committing them

to be justified, committing them to be sanctified;
made meet for life and for death, for time and
for eternity.* And there is no limit to this
deposit. All that belongs to them,—all their
cares and trials, sorrows and joys, crosses and
losses; the minutest accidents of their lot, as
well as the momentous crisis-hours of their history. He asks them to cast, not some of their
cares, or their weightier cares, but *all* their
cares. In Old Testament language, "He puts
their tears into His bottle." He counts their
sorrows, drop by drop, tear by tear. "He keeps
them as the apple of His eye;" what touches
them, touches *Him!*

Are we ready to subscribe also to this second
article in St Paul's dying creed? Are we
prepared to say, "I am persuaded He is able to
keep that which I have committed unto Him?"
With an unknown future before us, can we
exult in the thought, that though unknown to
us, it is known to Him, and in His hands we
can joyfully leave it? It may be different in-

---

* "The metaphor here is that of a pledge deposited, and the depositor *trusting* the depositary."— ALFORD's *Greek Test*.

deed, in one respect, with us, from what it was with the great Apostle. To him, the future was at this time a very limited one. One brief day and night might embrace it all. He was living at any moment expecting the summons, "Come up hither." But whether life with us may be long or short, how joyous to be able to feel that all (yes, *all*) is in His hands. Every arrangement regarding our temporal lot, and, better still, the deathless interests of the soul which He has purchased with His own blood. In giving Himself, He has given the pledge of every other blessing. And mark the beautiful combination in the text. It is not only Christ "able to keep ;"—(the consciousness of having a strong city in which salvation is appointed for walls and bulwarks ;) but within this citadel, we *know* Him who is the Keeper. He who is able to keep me, is a known, a tried, a trusted Saviour. An earthly stronghold may have massive walls and fortifications; but these, in themselves, are soulless, inanimate. They may have been built by the enemy. I may have no interest in being within them, or in retaining them; they are only fled to as a temporary shelter; not one living being I care for, may be there to cheer me. How different would be my feelings, if within that Castle's walls there were those who *knew* me—beloved friends, or brave comrades! How thrilling was that moment—the most touching in all our Indian rebellion—when that terrible fortress, within which hope, once and again sickened and died, was entered by the band of relieving heroes, amid the joyful tears of the beleaguered garrison, and brother and friend were locked in mutual embrace! Such is the believer's Gospel Citadel. Christ is a living Redeemer, a "living kinsman." He is not only "a stronghold in the day of trouble," but "He *knoweth* them that trust in Him" (Nahum i. 7). In leaning on His arm, it is not like the staff of the Pilgrim, a welcome support, but yet a dead, pulseless, lifeless thing, that can respond to no sympathy, and solace no sorrow. But it is the arm of a Friend: "Who is this that cometh up from the wilderness leaning upon her beloved?" Let us fearlessly entrust the keeping of our souls to Him in well-doing, as unto a faithful

Creator. Whatever be uncertain in the future, let us commend to His better wisdom, saying, "Not my will, but Thy will." "The Lord is thy *keeper;* the Lord is thy shade upon thy right hand. The sun shall not smite thee by day, nor the moon by night. The Lord shall preserve thee from all evil: He shall preserve thy soul."

III. We come now to the Apostle's glorious prospect of *a final day of triumph.* "*Against* THAT *day.*" "That day." When adverting to the same phrase last Sabbath, in his prayer for Onesiphorus, we noted the reiterated references made by St Paul to that significant era. We need not further dwell on its many suggestive themes for consideration. Let us only put the practical question, Are *we* in any similar measure "looking for and hasting unto the coming of the day of God?" Have we that day habitually before us, as it evidently was before the faithful of the Apostolic age? Are we longing for it, as the sailor for his port, or the Pilgrim for his home? When a brother or friend is expected from a distant land, how eagerly do we look for him!

How ardently does affection listen to every footfall on the street, or gaze wistfully on every sail as it appears on the distant line of blue sea? How does the mother deck out the chamber for her long absent son, with all the lavish ingenuity which love can devise, to give him a fond welcome? Are we thus longing for the return of this "Chiefest among ten thousand?" Are our hearts swept, and garnished, and beautified for His reception? Are we ready to echo the exulting words of the Psalmist—"Let the heavens rejoice, and let the earth be glad, let the sea roar, and the fulness thereof. Let the field be joyful, and all that is therein: then shall all the trees of the wood rejoice before the Lord: for He cometh, for He cometh to judge the earth?"

To those who cannot join in the Apostle's triumphant words—to those who are unmeet and unprepared for "that day," there is surely deep solemnity and awe in the prospect of it. St Paul, in another place, speaks of it "overtaking as a thief." It is "at midnight" the cry will be heard, "Behold, the Bridegroom cometh,"—the hour He is least looked for and least expected.

Brethren, it is not for us to know the times and seasons; when that trumpet shall sound, it is not for us presumptuously to predicate. But the day of our death is virtually to us 'the day of Christ's coming;' and as such, He *may* come soon; He *must* come at some time; He *will* come unexpectedly. When the river runs smoothest,—no dimple on its surface,—rock and tree and mountain mirrored in its bosom;—how often *then* is the waterfall at hand; and maddened into thunder, that river takes its leap into the dark caldron-depths below? So, often, when life appears most placid,—its sun shining, its green banks carpeted with flowers, its stream undimpled by one rippling wave, the great cataract of death is nigh, and with one giant bound it plunges into the abyss of eternity! How is it with us? Can we say with St Paul in this same Epistle, in the prospect of that day, "*I am now ready?*" Are we ready? Are we always ready? Is the step between us and death changed into the step between us and glory? the hour of our departure into the hour of victory? "Behold He cometh!" Would there be music in that word to us? Would we be ready with the response, "Lo, this is our God; we have waited for Him?" or would it rather find us on our knees with the reply, 'Not yet, not yet! Tarry, Lord! tarry! Yet a few more days, a few more weeks, a few more years—I am yet unprepared for the reckoning. He cometh! but for me, there is no pardon in His voice; for me, there is no mercy in His footstep. He cometh! but it will be "with flaming fire."' What is it that makes the thought of that day, and the meeting with the Judge, fearful? It is the sense of sin unforgiven. We never can endure to face a God unreconciled. So long as sin is not cancelled, and pardon through Christ neither sought nor secured; so long as passion is left to uncontrolled dominion, and holiness of heart and life are undesired and unattained; then, rather than breathe the Apostolic prayer, "Come, Lord Jesus," what would we not do to evade His glance? where would we not rush to avoid that withering rejection and disownment; gazing on injured Goodness and unrequited Love? God grant, that all of us may be able to "know whom we have believed" as Christ the Saviour, and then we shall not be ashamed to meet Him as Christ the Judge. If, I repeat, the hour of our departure from the world be really and virtually to us the hour of Christ's coming may we seek, now, so

> "To live, that when our summons comes to join
> The innumerable caravan, that moves
> To that mysterious realm, where each shall take
> His chamber in the silent halls of death;
> We go, not like the quarry slave at night
> Scourged to his dungeon; but, sustain'd and sooth'd
> By an unfaltering trust, approach our grave
> Like one who wraps the drapery of his couch
> About him, and lies down to pleasant dreams."

With the words of our text, the great drama of St Paul's great life closes. He has been well likened, at this hour, to the conqueror in the adjoining Capitol, waiting for the crown to be placed on his brow. The curtain falls, as he utters the dying testimony we have now been considering; and we are only left to imagine the rest:—The final trial in Nero's Basilica; the condemnation (if tradition can be trusted); the scourging, the few remaining days in the Mamertine, before passing to a more righteous judgment-seat; the farewell glimpses of beloved friends, among whom we can, only by doubtful surmise, include Luke, Timothy, Clemens, Linus, Pudens, Onesimus, Tychicus, Aristarchus, and possibly other representatives from the Palatine and Trastevere. We can further picture the band of Roman soldiers hurrying outside the Ostian Gate with their unresisting prisoner; wistful eyes following, in mute, expressive agony; the silence broken only by sobs and tears that dare not be repressed. Then the arrival at that solitary spot in the naked Campagna, which still retains the tradition of his beheading. Like his dear Lord before him, he has willingly borne his Cross "without the gate." The fatal weapon descends; and Angels are ready to conduct the soul of the glorious hero to Paradise. In the simple words of his beloved friend and contemporary, Clement, "So he departed from the world, and went to that holy place, having shown himself the noblest pattern of endurance." Even though we utterly reject the baseless fiction of the *Tre Fontane*, we may accept the beautiful truth it symbolises and adumbrates; that death was not—could not be, the close of a life like his. Though his lips were now irrevocably sealed, Fountains of "grace, and mercy, and peace" (Heaven's threefold benediction he had so often uttered), were left to well up, fresh and copious as ever, to bless, in all coming centuries, that world he had made perpetual debtor by his teaching and example. A glorious sun had set,—vanished behind the horizon in golden glory; but the mountain-peaks of all ages are still lighted up with its undying radiance: "He being dead, yet speaketh." The saddest moment to the mourning Church on earth (for she had sustained no such loss since the departure of her Great Head) ushered the martyred Apostle into the blissful and merited scene of recompense for all his sufferings and labours. What one so often reads, in the rude inscriptions traced by fond hands on the tombs in the Catacombs, had in his case their truest, fullest, most sacred meaning and significance, "IN CHRISTO IN PACE":—

> "The pains of death are past :
> Labour and sorrow cease :
> And life's long warfare closed at last,
> His soul is found IN PEACE."

Whether, indeed, he really sleeps in the spot where tradition has deposited his ashes, we cannot positively affirm. But the rearers of the magnificent mausoleum, which, with its aureole of lighted lamps, enshrines his memory, have selected, at all events, the most appropriate of epitaphs in those simple words we have more than once spoken of in their connection with that place—

"TO ME TO LIVE IS CHRIST, AND TO DIE IS GAIN."

Following, as we have been endeavouring to do (we trust not without interest), the footsteps of the great Apostle in this ancient capital of the world, may it be our joy to meet him at last in the true *"Eternal City,"*—"the city which hath foundations," and there testify the debt which, under God, we owe to him in common with the millions on millions who on earth have read, and prayed, and rejoiced over his utterances. It was one of the illustrious Chrysostom's bright anticipations of Heaven (may we be able in some feeble measure to participate in the prospect): "If not standing near him, yet see him we certainly shall, glistening near the throne of the King, where the cherubim sing the glory; where the seraphim are flying; there we shall see PAUL, as a chief and leader of the choir of the Saints, and shall enjoy his generous love."

I can only appropriately conclude with the final ascription of the now sainted Apostle, addressed to believers in ROME, as contained in the closing verses of his own Epistle to the Romans (xvi. 25, 27):—

"NOW TO HIM
THAT IS OF POWER TO STABLISH YOU
ACCORDING TO MY GOSPEL,
AND THE PREACHING OF JESUS CHRIST:

. . . .

TO GOD ONLY WISE
BE GLORY, THROUGH JESUS CHRIST, FOR EVER.
AMEN."

PRINTED BY BALLANTYNE AND COMPANY
EDINBURGH AND LONDON

WORKS

BY THE

REV. J. R. MACDUFF, D.D.

RECENTLY PUBLISHED,

Fifth Thousand,

MEMORIES OF PATMOS;

OR,

SOME OF THE GREAT WORDS AND VISIONS OF THE APOCALYPSE.

Post 8vo, 6s. 6d. cloth.

"Dr Macduff does not attempt to enter into all the minutiæ of prophetical interpretation in this volume. He singles out for consideration some of the most remarkable and sublime passages, and expounds them with much force, and with all that wealth of poetic and tender language which has always characterised his writings."—*Record.*

"The force and eloquence of many passages in the volume could scarcely be surpassed."—*Our Own Fireside.*

"In Dr Macduff's own attractive style, he writes on these themes a great deal that is in the highest sense edifying and consolatory. It is a book which all Christians will read with advantage."—*Evangelical Magazine.*

"The rich eloquence of Dr Macduff, his powers of graphic description and wealth of illustration, are well known, and have never been more suitably employed than in commending to the attention of Christians the grand lessons of the Apocalypse."—*Christian Advocate.*

Tenth Thousand, small crown 8vo, 3s. 6d. cloth,

THE SHEPHERD AND HIS FLOCK;

Or, The Keeper of Israel and the Sheep of His Pasture.

With Vignette.

"This is a remarkably well-written volume, eminently practical and devout in its tone, and one which spiritually-minded persons will read with pleasure and profit. . . . It is, we think, quite equal to the most popular of the productions of the same gifted and useful writer."—*Journal of Sacred Literature.*

"The volume deserves, and it cannot fail of finding, a very cordial reception in every section of the Church of Christ."—*British Standard.*

"Written in Dr Macduff's peculiar style of simplicity, eloquence, and unction."—*British Quarterly Review.*

"Dr Macduff's present work is equal to the best of his former ones. The subject is peculiarly adapted for the author's imaginative style; and the reader peruses chapter after chapter struck by the rich fund of apposite illustration—drawn both from nature and revelation—with which he throws fresh light upon it, the quiet and affectionate appeals with which he urges its lessons, and the fine vein of Christian thought and feeling which pervades every page. It is a most delightful volume, and the publishers have done their part to make it a handsome one."—*Daily Review.*

Eighth Thousand, crown 8vo, 3s. 6d. cloth,

NOONTIDE AT SYCHAR;

Or, The Story of Jacob's Well.

"The exposition is characterised by the author's well-known style, matter, and manner of handling. It is poetic throughout, and will detract nothing from his well-earned and well-established position as a graceful, pious, and pleasant writer, who makes the old things new."—*Weekly Review.*

Sixth Thousand, post 8vo, 6s. 6d. cloth,

MEMORIES OF OLIVET.

"The almost photographic clearness with which every point around Jerusalem is described, and the frequent though unobtrusive illustration of the sacred text from Eastern life, together with the vivid realisation of the movements of our Saviour during the last few days of His earthly career, make the 'Memories of Olivet' a most valuable companion in the study of the preacher and teacher, and in the chamber of the home student."—*Record.*

Eighth Thousand, post 8vo, 6s. 6d. cloth,

THE PROPHET OF FIRE;

Or, The Life and Times of Elijah, with their Lessons.

"To the execution of his task, Dr Macduff brings a rich stock of wisdom and knowledge, sacred and secular, which he employs with the utmost skill in the elucidation of the character of Elijah, and the circumstances under which he fulfilled his mission."—*Christian Times.*

"The life of Elijah, 'the grandest and most romantic character that Israel ever produced,' is just the thing for Dr Macduff's artistic eye and graphic pen."—*Glasgow Herald.*

Sixteenth Thousand, post 8vo, 6s. 6d. cloth,

SUNSETS ON THE HEBREW MOUNTAINS

Being some of the more Prominent Biographies of Sacred Story Viewed from Life's Close.

"Dr Macduff has rightly appreciated the characters he has described, and has truthfully delineated their features. The points of instruction, too, which he draws from them are apposite, scriptural, and telling."—*Church of England Magazine.*

"Clear and instructive."—*British Standard.*

"The title of this beautiful and interesting volume is fanciful. We heartily commend it to all our readers for its piety, thoughtfulness, and beauty."—*Patriot.*

Twenty-first Thousand, post 8vo, 6s. 6d. cloth,

MEMORIES OF GENNESARET;

Or, Our Lord's Ministrations by the Sea of Galilee.

"An excellent and exceeding attractive work. Its character is simplicity, earnestness, and devoutness."—*Witness.*

"This book contains more than twenty chapters on events and teachings connected with the beautiful Lake of Gennesaret—sojournings, journeys, miracles, discourses, parables, all set forth in the author's well-known and justly-winning manner. We commend what he writes to all who prize evangelical truth delivered with sacred unction."—*Rev. Dr Alexander of New York.*

Forty-first Thousand,

MEMORIES OF BETHANY;

Or, Our Lord's Sympathy with the Sick and Sorrowful.

Crown 8vo, 3s. 6d. cloth.

Twenty-ninth Thousand, Revised,

THE FOOTSTEPS OF ST PAUL:

Being a Life of the Apostle. Designed for Youth.

With Illustrations, crown 8vo, 5s. cloth.

Fourteenth Thousand,

GRAPES OF ESHCOL;

Or, Gleanings from the Land of Promise :

Being Meditations on Heaven, for every day of the month.

Crown 8vo, 3s. 6d. cloth.

Sixteenth Thousand,

THE HART AND THE WATER-BROOKS:
A Practical Exposition of the Forty-Second Psalm.

Crown 8vo, 3s. 6d. cloth.

Thirty-first Thousand,

A VOLUME OF FAMILY PRAYERS.
Crown 8vo, 3s. 6d. cloth.

Seventh Thousand,

THE STORY OF BETHLEHEM:
A Book for Children. With Illustrations by THOMAS.

Crown 8vo, 2s. 6d. cloth.

Seventh Thousand,

CURFEW CHIMES;
Or, Thoughts for Life's Eventide.

16mo, 1s. 6d. cloth.

Three Hundred and Fifty-sixth Thousand,

MORNING AND NIGHT WATCHES.
16mo, 1s. 6d. cloth ; or, separately, 32mo, 8d. sewed, 1s. cloth.

Large Type, crown 8vo, 3s. 6d. cloth.

Two Hundred and Sixth Thousand,

THE MIND AND WORDS OF JESUS.

16mo, 1s. 6d. cloth, or, separately, 32mo, 8d. sewed, 1s. cloth.

Thirty-seventh Thousand,

THE THOUGHTS OF GOD.

16mo, 1s. 6d. cloth.

Twelfth Thousand,

THE THOUGHTS OF GOD, AND THE WORDS OF JESUS.

In one vol. 16mo, 2s. 6d. cloth.

Fourth Thousand,

ALTAR INCENSE:

BEING MORNING WATCHES, EVENING INCENSE, AND ALTAR STONES.

A Manual of Devotion for Morning and Evening.

16mo, 2s. 6d. cloth.

Sixth Thousand,

THE WOODCUTTER OF LEBANON:

A Story Illustrative of a Jewish Institution.

16mo, 2s. cloth.

Eighth Thousand,
THE CITIES OF REFUGE;
Or, The Name of Jesus. A Sunday Book for the Young.

16mo, 1s. 6d. cloth.

Ninety-eighth Thousand,
THE BOW IN THE CLOUD;
Or, Words of Comfort for Hours of Sorrow.

32mo, 8d, sewed, 1s. cloth.

Thirty-fourth Thousand,
EVENING INCENSE.

32mo, 8d. sewed, 1s. cloth.

THE FAITHFUL PROMISER, AND THE MORNING AND NIGHT WATCHES.

In one vol. 16mo, 2s, cloth.

FERGUS MORTON;
Or, The Story of a Scottish Boy.

16mo, 9d. cloth.

Nineteenth Thousand,

ALTAR STONES:

Original Hymns for Plain Readers.

16mo, 6d. sewed, 8d. cloth.

Fourteenth Thousand,

THE FIRST BEREAVEMENT;

Or, Words Addressed to a Mourner on the Occasion of a First Trial.

32mo, 4d. sewed, 6d. cloth.

Eighth Thousand,

WILLOWS BY THE WATERCOURSES;

Or, God's Promises to the Young.

64mo, 3d. sewed, 6d. cloth.

New Edition, revised and corrected,

THE EXILES OF LUCERNA;

Or, The Sufferings of the Waldenses during the Persecution of 1686.

16mo, 2s. 6d. cloth.

LONDON: JAMES NISBET & CO., 21 BERNERS STREET, W.

December, 1871.

A SELECTION FROM
JAMES NISBET AND CO.'S
LIST OF PUBLICATIONS.

LIGHT AND TRUTH. Bible Thoughts and Themes. Fifth and concluding volume. The Revelation of St. John. By the Rev. HORATIUS BONAR, D.D. Crown 8vo, 5s. cloth.

THE IRON HORSE; or, Life on the Line. A Railway Tale. By R. M. BALLANTYNE, author of "The Lifeboat," &c. With Illustrations. Crown 8vo, 5s. cloth.

ST. PAUL IN ROME; or, the Teachings, Fellowships, and Dying Testimony of the great Apostle in the City of the Cæsars. Being Sermons preached in Rome during the Spring of 1871. With a copious Introduction, containing details, Local, Historical, and Legendary, gathered on the spot. By the Rev. J. R. MACDUFF, D.D. With Photograph. Small crown 8vo, 4s. 6d. cloth.

A FOURTH EDITION OF THE EXPLANATORY AND PRACTICAL COMMENTARY ON THE NEW TESTAMENT; intended chiefly as a Help to Family Devotion. Edited and continued by the Rev. W. DALTON, B.D. Two volumes, 8vo, 24s. cloth.

INCIDENTS IN THE LIFE AND MINISTRY OF THE REV. A. R. C. DALLAS, M.A., RECTOR OF WONSTON. By HIS WIDOW. With Portrait. Demy 8vo, 10s. 6d. cloth.

STORIES OF VINEGAR HILL. Illustrative of the Parable of the Sower. By the author of "The Golden Ladder." With coloured Illustrations. Small crown 8vo, 3s. 6d. cloth.

THE HOUSE IN TOWN. A sequel to "Opportunities." By the author of "The Wide Wide World," &c. With coloured Illustrations. Small crown 8vo, 2s. 6d. cloth.

THE CULTURE OF PLEASURE; or, The Enjoyment of Life in its Social and Religious Aspects. By the author of "The Mirage of Life." Crown 8vo, 6s. cloth.

SYNOPTICAL LECTURES ON THE BOOKS OF HOLY SCRIPTURE. First Series—Genesis to Canticles. By the Rev. DONALD FRASER, M.A. Post 8vo, 6s. cloth.
"Singularly interesting instructive, and comprehensive lectures."—*Record*.

MEMORY'S PICTURES. Poems by the author of "Memorials of Capt. Hedley Vicars," &c. Foolscap 8vo, 2s. 6d. cloth, gilt edges.

"A most elegant and attractive volume of poetry."—*Scattered Nation.*

DRAYTON HALL. Stories Illustrative of the Beatitudes. By the author of "Nettie's Mission," &c. With coloured Illustrations. Small crown 8vo, 3s. 6d. cloth.

"A pleasant book for boys."—*Literary World.*

WITHOUT AND WITHIN. A New England Story. With coloured Illustrations. Small crown 8vo, 3s. 6d. cloth.

"The story is well told; the characters are well delineated; the pathetic and the humorous are skilfully blended."—*Maryland Church Record.*

JOHN OF THE GOLDEN MOUTH. A Life of Chrysostom, Preacher of Antioch, and Primate of Constantinople. By the Rev. W. MACGILVRAY, D.D. Post 8vo, 6s. cloth.

"A full, fresh, instructive, and interesting narrative."—*Weekly Review.*

THE DAY OF BEREAVEMENT; Its Lessons and its Consolations. By G. W. MYLNE, Author of "Reposing in Jesus," &c. 16mo, 1s. 6d. cloth.

"Words *from* the heart, which will reach *to* the heart."—*Our Own Fireside.*

THE TIMES OF THE GENTILES; Being the 2520 Years from the First Year of Nebuchadnezzar (B.C. 623) to the 1260th Year of the Mohammedan Treading Down of Jerusalem, A.D. 1896. By the Rev. J. BAYLEE, D.D. Post 8vo, 5s. cloth.

"This book is fresh, and full of acute remark and pointed criticism on Scripture."—*Journal of Prophecy.*

EPISTOLA CONSOLATORIA. By JUAN PEREZ, one of the Spanish Reformers in the Sixteenth Century. With a Life of the Author, by the late B. W. WIFFEN. Small crown 8vo, 3s. 6d. cloth.

"There is more of God's word in the book than the author's; and its child-like devotional spirit will commend it always to the sorrowful."—*British and Foreign Evangelical Review.*

AN ENQUIRY INTO THE CHRISTIAN LAW AS TO THE RELATIONSHIPS WHICH BAR MARRIAGE. By the late Professor W. LINDSAY, D.D. Small Crown 8vo, 2s. 6d. cloth.

"Dr. Lindsay is an able, acute, and logical reasoner."—*Record.*
"Model of controversial discussion."—*Presbyterian.*

HYMNS AND SONGS OF PILGRIM LIFE; or, Steps to the Throne. By the Rev. J. GANN, B.A., Bulmer. Small crown 8vo, 2s. 6d. cloth.

"Worth reading—more than can be said of much modern poetry."—*Scattered Nation.*
"A collection of hymns and songs, many of them very sweet."—*Weekly Review.*

THE KING'S TABLE. The Lord's Supper in Letters
to a Young Friend. By the Rev. G. PHILLIP, M.A., Edinburgh. 16mo, 8d. sewed, 1s. cloth.

"We do not aver that the little treatise before us has reached perfection, but it comes nearer the mark than anything we have lately met with."—*British and Foreign Evangelical Review.*

MEMORIES OF PATMOS; or, Some of the Great
Words and Visions of the Apocalypse. By the Rev. J. R. MACDUFF, D.D. With Vignette. Post 8vo, 6s. cloth.

"Dr. Macduff has given us a volume of beautiful thoughts, and has clothed these thoughts with language which is at once elegant and forcible."—*Rock.*

MOSES THE MAN OF GOD. A Series of Lectures
by the late JAMES HAMILTON, D.D., F.L.S. Small Crown 8vo, 5s., cloth.

"Graceful description, imaginative reconstruction, unconventional, and often very ingenious, sometimes learned disquisition, with the light graceful touch of poetic style and delicate fancy."—*British Quarterly Review.*

LAYS OF THE HOLY LAND. Selected from Ancient
and Modern Poets by the Rev. HORATIUS BONAR, D.D. New Edition, with Illustrations from original Photographs and Drawings. Crown 4to, 12s., cloth.

"The Holy Land is a subject to which all great poets have devoted some of their best endeavours, and these are now brought together and adorned by illustrations worthy of such a text. . . . The volume will long remain a favourite."—*Times.*

THE FLOATING LIGHT OF THE GOODWIN
SANDS. A Tale by R. M. BALLANTYNE, Author of "The Lifeboat," &c. With Illustrations. Crown 8vo, 5s. cloth.

"As full of incident, as healthy in tone, and as fresh and vigorous in style as any of its predecessors."—*Scotsman.*

A MISSIONARY OF THE APOSTOLIC SCHOOL.
Being the Life of Dr. Judson, of Burmah. Revised and Edited by the Rev. HORATIUS BONAR, D.D. Small Crown 8vo, 3s. 6d., cloth.

"Very well written."—*Daily Review.*   "Every way readable."—*Nonconformist.*

LITTLE ELSIE'S SUMMER AT MALVERN. By
the Hon. Mrs. CLIFFORD BUTLER. Royal 16mo, 2s.6d. cloth. With Illustrations.

"A pleasing little story."—*Daily Telegraph.*

TOILING IN ROWING; or, Half-hours of Earnest Con-
verse with my Hard-working Friends. By one who knows and loves them. Small Crown 8vo, 2s., cloth limp.

"An earnest, affectionate, and practical little book."—*Daily Review.*

A HISTORY OF THE REFORMATION FOR
CHILDREN. By the Rev. E. NANGLE, B.A. With Illustrations. Three Volumes, 16mo, 4s. 6d. cloth.

PLEASANT FRUITS FROM THE COTTAGE AND
THE CLASS. By MARIA V. G. HAVERGAL. Small Crown 8vo, 2s. 6d. cloth limp, 3s. cloth boards.

"Will be read with profit and delight."—*Our Own Fireside.*
"Peculiarly well suited for reading at District and Mothers' Meetings, &c."—*Church of England S. S. Magazine.*

WHAT SHE COULD, AND OPPORTUNITIES TO
DO IT. By the Author of "The Wide Wide World." With Coloured Illustrations. Small Crown 8vo, 3s. 6d. cloth.

"A capital book for girls."—*Daily Review.*
"Clever and interesting little book."—*Glasgow Herald.*

FAITHFUL UNTO DEATH; or, Susine and Claude of
the Val Pelice. By ANNA CAROLINA DI TERGOLINA. With Coloured Illustrations. Fcap. 8vo, 2s. 6d. cloth.

"Full of a pathos which will entrance the youthful reader."—*Weekly Review.*

GLEN LUNA; or, Dollars and Cents. By ANNA WARNER,
Author of "The Golden Ladder." New Edition. With Coloured Illustrations. Small Crown 8vo, 3s. 6d. cloth.

"A really good tale."—*Rock.*
"Sure to increase in popularity."—*English Presbyterian Messenger*

LOVE FULFILLING THE LAW. Stories on the
Commandments. 16mo, 2s. 6d. cloth.

"Pretty and handy little book."—*Glasgow Herald.*

A PRACTICAL COMMENTARY ON THE GOSPEL
ACCORDING TO ST. JOHN. In simple and familiar language. By G. D. Small Crown 8vo, 3s. 6d. cloth.

"We cordially recommend them as truly simple, earnest, and faithful comments."—*Our Own Fireside.*

NOTES OF OPEN-AIR SERMONS. By the Rev.
EDWARD WALKER, D.C.L., Rector of Cheltenham. Edited by a Member of the Congregation. Small Crown 8vo, 1s. 6d., cloth limp.

"Models of sound, faithful, and affectionate gospel preaching."—*English Presbyterian Messenger.*

THE ATONEMENT; in its Relations to the Covenant, the
Priesthood, and the Intercession of our Lord. By the Rev. HUGH MARTIN, M.A. Post 8vo, 6s. cloth.

"A volume written with remarkable vigour and earnestness."—*British Quarterly Review.*
"Well worthy of a careful perusal, and we cordially recommend it to all our readers, and especially to ministers and students of theology."—*Evangelical Witness.*

THE SCRIPTURAL ACCOUNT OF CREATION
VINDICATED BY THE TEACHING OF SCIENCE: or, A New Method of Reconciling the Mosaic and Geological Records of Creation. By the Rev. WM. PAUL, D.D. Post 8vo, 5s. cloth.

"Dr. Paul is entitled to the highest commendation for the extent and accuracy of his knowledge, and for the able, modest, and candid manner in which he applies it to his argument."—*Presbyterian.*

THE LIFE OF THE LATE JAMES HAMILTON,
D.D., F.L.S. By the Rev. WILLIAM ARNOT, Edinburgh. Post 8vo, 7s. 6d. cloth. With Portrait.
"We rejoice to recommend this volume as a congenial and worthy record of one of the noblest and most fruitful lives with which the Church of Christ has been blessed in modern days. The editor's work has been done with admirable judgment."
—*Weekly Review.*

A MEMOIR OF THE LATE REV. WILLIAM C.
BURNS, M.A., Missionary to China. By Professor ISLAY BURNS, D.D., Glasgow. Crown 8vo, 6s. cloth. With Portrait.
" A more apostolic life has rarely been spent. . . . It is impossible to estimate too highly the good that may flow from this record of Christian life and labour."
—*Sunday Magazine.*

THE LORD'S PRAYER. Lectures by the Rev. ADOLPH
SAPHIR, B.A., Greenwich. Small Crown 8vo, 5s. cloth.
"A work so wide in its range of thought, and so concentrated in its doctrinal teachings, so rich and well packed, yet so simple and interesting, and so clear, pure, and intelligible in expression does not often make its appearance."—*Christian Work.*

CHRIST IN THE WORD. By the Rev. FREDERICK
WHITFIELD, M.A., Author of "Voices from the Valley," &c. Small Crown 8vo, 3s. 6d. cloth.
"Very able and searching applications of spiritual truth."—*Our Own Fireside.*
"Excellent reading for the closet and family circle."—*Watchman.*

THE SHEPHERD AND HIS FLOCK; or, The Keeper
of Israel and the Sheep of His Pasture. By the Rev. J. R. MACDUFF, D.D. With Vignette. Small Crown 8vo, 3s. 6d. cloth.
"A remarkably well-written volume, eminently practical and devout in its tone, and one which spiritually-minded persons will read with both pleasure and profit."—*Journal of Sacred Literature.*

ERLING THE BOLD. A Tale of the Norse Sea-Kings.
By R. M. BALLANTYNE, Author of "The Lifeboat," &c. With Illustrations by the Author. Crown 8vo, 5s. cloth.
"The story is cleverly designed, and abounds with elements of romantic interest; and the author's illustrations are scarcely less vigorous than his text."—*Athenæum.*

LIGHT AND TRUTH. Bible Thoughts and Themes—
First, Second, Third, and Fourth Series — 1. THE OLD TESTAMENT. 2. THE GOSPELS. 3. THE ACTS AND THE LARGER EPISTLES. 4. THE LESSER EPISTLES. 5. THE REVELATION OF ST. JOHN. By the Rev. HORATIUS BONAR, D.D. Crown 8vo, each 5s. cloth.
"Rich in matter and very suggestive."—*Christian Advocate.*
"Valuable work. It contains a series of brief expositions well suited for private use, or for family reading."—*Record.*

LECTURES ON HOSEA XIV. Preached in Portman
Chapel during Lent, 1869. By the Rev. J. W. REEVE, M.A. Small Crown 8vo, 3s. 6d. cloth.
"It would be hard to over-estimate the amount of Gospel truth, practical exhortation, plain speaking, and affectionate interest in the spiritual welfare of his people, contained in these six lectures."—*Record.*

HE THAT OVERCOMETH; or, A Conquering Gospel. By the Rev. W. E. BOARDMAN, M.A., Author of "The Higher Christian Life," &c. Small Crown 8vo, 3s. 6d. cloth.

"It is an excellent book for reading out on the Sabbath evenings in the family circle."—*Christian Work.*

THE SPANISH BARBER. A Tale, by the Author of "Mary Powell." Small Crown 8vo, 3s. 6d. cloth.

"A charming story for young and old, and most charmingly told."—*Rock.*
"An instructive story of missionary work in Spain."—*Christian Advocate.*

SERMONS. Preached at King's Lynn. By the late Rev. E. L. HULL, B.A. First and Second Series. Post 8vo, each 6s. cloth.

"This new volume of twenty sermons has all the claims of the first—the same happy use of Scripture, the same clear and firm grasp of the principle of every text he selected, the same earnest longing after the beauty and holiness on which he has now entered, the same play of imagination, the same freshness of thought, and fitness of utterance."—*Freeman.*

THE TITLES OF OUR LORD; A Series of Sketches for Every Sunday in the Christian Year, to be used in Bible-Class, Sunday School, and Private Study. By the Rev. ROWLEY HILL, M.A., Vicar of Frant. 16mo, 1s. 6d. cloth.

"The idea is excellent. . . . The matter is well arranged, free from repetitions, and in exposition thoroughly scriptural."—*Record.*

HEADS AND TALES; Or, Anecdotes and Stories of Quadrupeds and other Beasts. Compiled by ADAM WHITE, Duddingston. Second Edition. With Illustrations. Small Crown 8vo, 3s. 6d. cloth.

"Full of pleasant anecdotes."—*Times.*
"Amusing, instructive, and interesting."—*Standard.*

STEPPING HEAVENWARD. By Mrs. PRENTISS. Author of "Little Susy's Six Birthdays," &c. With Coloured Illustrations. Small Crown 8vo, 2s. 6d. cloth.

"A faithful diary, recording the experiences of a good and gentle soul in its onward march to a better land."—*Rock.*

THE ROMANCE OF NATURAL HISTORY. First and Second Series. By. P. H. GOSSE, F.R.S. With many Illustrations. Post 8vo, each 7s. 6d. cloth; cheap edition, Small Crown 8vo, each 3s. 6d. cloth.

"A very pleasing and attractive work."—*Times.*
"It would be difficult to find more attractive gift books for the young."—*Record.*

BOOKS FOR WAYFARERS. By ANNA WARNER, Author of the "Golden Ladder." 32mo, cloth. 1. WAYFARING HYMNS, ORIGINAL AND SELECTED. 6d. 2. THE MELODY OF THE TWENTY-THIRD PSALM. 8d.

"There is an unction and a beauty about the books that well fit them to be pocket or table companions."—*Freeman.*
"Two little books, beautiful without and within."—*English Presbyterian Messenger.*

MEMORIALS OF THE LATE JAMES HENDERSON, M.D., F.R.C.S.E. Medical Missionary to China. With Appendix. Small Crown 8vo, 3s. 6d. cloth. With Portrait. Also, Cheap and Abridged Edition, 16mo, 1s. cloth limp.

"The memorials of Dr. Henderson form as beautiful and exhilarating a little history as it has been for some time our task or pleasure to read. . . . . It is the story of one of those noble lives before which power and difficulty recoil, and give up the contest."—*Eclectic Review.*

MEMOIR AND REMAINS OF THE LATE REV. JAMES D. BURNS, M.A., of Hampstead. By the late Rev. Dr. HAMILTON. With Portrait. Small Crown 8vo, 5s. cloth.

"It is not often that such sympathy of piety, friendship, and genius, exists between a biographer and his subject. It makes the book very precious—a memorial of the one as much as the other."—*British Quarterly Review.*

NOONTIDE AT SYCHAR; or, The Story of Jacob's Well. By the Rev. J. R. MACDUFF, D.D. With Vignettes. Small Crown 8vo, 3s. 6d. cloth.

"One of the most attractive of the many pleasant and profitable religious studies published by Dr. Macduff."—*Daily Review.*

DEEP DOWN. A Tale of the Cornish Mines. By R. M. BALLANTYNE, Author of "The Life Boat," etc. With Illustrations. Small Crown 8vo, 5s. cloth.

"This is just the subject for Mr. Ballantyne, whose stories in connection with that enterprise and adventure which have made England great are amongst the best of modern days."—*Daily News.*

FAMILY PRAYERS FOR FOUR WEEKS. With Additional Prayers for Especial Days and Occasions. By the Very Rev. HENRY LAW, M.A., Dean of Gloucester. Small Crown 8vo, 3s. 6d. cloth.

"Thoroughly sound and scriptural, and really devotional."—*Christian Observer.*

LIFE OF THE LATE REV. JOHN MILNE, M.A., of Perth. By the Rev. HORATIUS BONAR, D.D. With Portrait. Crown 8vo, 6s. cloth.

"Written with the elegance, sound judgment, and good feeling which were to be expected from Dr. Bonar; and being given to a large extent in the autobiographical form, it is, on that account, the more trustworthy and valuable."—*British and Foreign Evangelical Review.*

A COMMENTARY ON ST. PAUL'S EPISTLE TO THE GALATIANS. With Sermons on the Principal Topics contained in it. By the Rev. EMILIUS BAYLEY, B.D., Vicar of St. John's, Paddington. Crown 8vo, 7s. 6d. cloth.

"Admirable commentary. It is full of well arranged and well digested matter, and without any pedantry, it is scholarlike in its criticisms."—*Record.*

TALES FROM ALSACE; or, Scenes and Portraits from
Life in the Days of the Reformation, as drawn from Old Chronicles. Translated from the German. Crown 8vo, 3s. 6d. cloth.

"We have not for a long time perused a more delightful book. . . . . we are certain wherever it is read it will be a great favourite with young and old."—*Daily Review.*

A MEMOIR OF THE LATE REV. DR. MALAN,
OF GENEVA. By one of his Sons. With Portrait and Engravings. Post 8vo, 7s. 6d. cloth

"We feel ourselves in this biography brought into contact with an humble but truly saintly man, whom to know is to love, and whom it is impossible to know without being ourselves benefited."—*Christian Work.*

FAMILY PRAYERS FOR A MONTH, with a few
Prayers for Special occasions. By the Rev. J. W. REEVE, M.A., Portman Chapel. Small Crown 8vo, 3s. 6d. cloth.

"Admirably suited for the devotions of a Christian household."—*Rock.*

BEACONS OF THE BIBLE. By the Very Rev. HENRY
LAW, M.A., Dean of Gloucester, Author of "Christ is All," etc. Small Crown 8vo, 3s. 6d. cloth.

"Dr. Law's work overflows with striking and beautiful images, briefly expressed in short, incisive sentences, often musical in their cadence, and melodious as poetry itself."—*Rock.*

THE WORKS OF THE LATE JAMES HAMILTON,
D.D., F.L.S. Complete in Six Vols., post 8vo, each 7s. 6d. cloth.

"More than most men he has embalmed his qualities in his writings. . . . They well deserve to be published in a permanent form, and this handsome library edition will be a great boon to many families."—*Freeman.*

OUR FATHER IN HEAVEN. The Lord's Prayer
Familiarly Explained and Illustrated. A Book for the Young. By the Rev. J. H. WILSON, Edinburgh. With Illustrations. Small Crown 8vo, 2s. 6d. cloth.

"We know no better book of its kind."—*Edinburgh Evening Courant.*

"One of the most interesting and successful expositions of the Lord's Prayer in our language."—*Evangelical Magazine.*

RIGHTS AND WRONGS; or, Begin at Home. By M. M.
GORDON, Author of "Work; Plenty to Do, and How to Do it." Small Crown 8vo, 2s. 6d. limp cloth.

"The purpose of the publication is for circulation amongst the female inmates of cottages and working men's houses, or to be read at mothers' or daughters' meetings. For these ends it will be found exceedingly suitable, and fitted to be widely useful."—*Aberdeen Free Press.*

FROM SEVENTEEN TO THIRTY. The Town Life
of a Youth from the Country; its Trials, Temptations, and Advantages. Lessons from the History of Joseph. By the Rev. THOMAS BINNEY. Small Crown 8vo, 1s. 6d. cloth.

"Nothing can exceed the quiet dignity, beauty, and simplicity of style in which this book is written. Not only is it a model of wise scriptural exposition, but we cannot at this moment recall anything that approaches it."—*English Independent.*

JAMES NISBET AND CO. 9

THE SABBATH-SCHOOL INDEX. Pointing out the
History and Progress of Sunday Schools, with approved modes of Instruction, etc., etc. By R. G. PARDEE, A.M. With Introductory Preface by the Rev. J. H. WILSON, Edinburgh. Small Crown 8vo, 2s. 6d. cloth.

"The author has succeeded in an admirable manner in producing a work that will stand pre-eminently as the teacher's handbook. We have not found one subject of any importance to the teacher which he has not considered."—*Weekly Review.*

MEMORIES OF OLIVET. By the Rev. J. R. MACDUFF,
D.D. With Vignette. Post 8vo, 6s. 6d. cloth.

"The almost photographic clearness with which every point around Jerusalem is described, and the frequent though unobtrusive illustration of the sacred text from eastern life, together with the vivid realization of the movements of our Saviour during the last few days of his earthly career, make the *Memories of Olivet* a most valuable companion in the study of the preacher and teacher, and in the chamber of the home student."—*Record.*

THE LIFE OF THE LATE REV. DR. MARSH,
of Beddington. By his DAUGHTER, the Author of "English Hearts and English Hands," etc. With Portrait. Post 8vo, 10s. cloth; Cheap Edition, Small Crown 8vo, 3s. 6d. cloth.

"We have read this volume with much interest, and can recommend it as an excellent account of Dr. Marsh's life and career, and of the associations connected with them."—*Times.*

MEMORIES OF GENNESARET; or, Our Lord's Minis-
trations in Galilee. With a new and extended Preface, from observations made upon the spot. By the Rev. J. R. MACDUFF, D.D. Post 8vo, 6s. 6d. cloth.

"An excellent and exceedingly attractive work. Its character is simplicity, earnestness, and devotedness."—*Witness.*

THE PEARL OF PARABLES. Notes on the Parable
of the Prodigal Son. By the late JAMES HAMILTON, D.D. With Twelve Illustrations by SELOUS. Printed on toned paper, and elegantly bound. Small 4to, 8s. 6d. cloth. Also a Cheap Edition, without Plates, 16mo, 1s. 6d. cloth.

"A book like this is a very rich enjoyment for both mind and heart. A more fitting gift-book for young men could hardly be conceived."—*British Quarterly Review.*

THE DARWINIAN THEORY OF THE TRANSMU-
TATION OF SPECIES EXAMINED. By a GRADUATE OF THE UNIVERSITY OF CAMBRIDGE. Demy 8vo, 10s. 6d. cloth.

"The volume is a work of no ordinary merit. . . . It indicates extensive reading, intimate acquaintance with the whole history of the Transmutation school of thinking, great mastery of the abundant material placed at the disposal of the author, and a large infusion of common sense."—*British Quarterly Review.*

PLAIN SERMONS ON THE GOSPEL MIRACLES.
By the Rev. ARTHUR ROBERTS, M.A. Crown 8vo, 5s. cloth.

"Plain and simple, without attempt at critical disquisition or philosophical inquiry, they are earnest, scriptural, and attractive. The style, with nothing lofty in it, is pleasant, and the sermons are thoroughly readable."—*Church of England Magazine.*

WORKS PUBLISHED BY

THE SHADOW AND THE SUBSTANCE. A Second Series of Addresses by STEVENSON A. BLACKWOOD, Esq. Small Crown 8vo. 2s. cloth limp, 2s. 6d. cloth boards.

"A very thoughtful and thoroughly scriptural view of the Passover. . . . To those who wish for useful reading to adult classes, or to mothers' meetings, we commend this book."—*Record.*

THE PROPHET OF FIRE; or, The Life and Times of Elijah, and their Lessons. By the Rev. J. R. MACDUFF, D.D. Post 8vo, 6s. 6d. cloth.

"Full of incident, rich in illustration, smooth and pleasing in style, and abounding in practical lessons."—*English Presbyterian Messenger.*

THE PRAISE-BOOK; being "Hymns of Praise," with accompanying Tunes. By the Rev. W. REID, M.A. Harmonies written or revised by H. E. DIBDIN. Crown 4to. 7s. 6d. cloth elegant.

"This magnificent volume has no rival, at least we know of none published in England. It is a standard book both as to hymns and music."—*Sword and Trowel.*

ST. PAUL; His Life and Ministry to the Close of his Third Missionary Journey. By the Rev. THOMAS BINNEY. Crown 8vo, 5s. cloth.

"Mr. Binney has elaborated into a volume his magnificent lectures on St. Paul's Life and Ministry. . . . Mr. Binney's books need no commendation of ours."—*Quarterly Messenger Young Men's Christian Association.*

SUNSETS ON THE HEBREW MOUNTAINS; or, Some of the most prominent Biographies of Sacred Story viewed from Life's Close. By the Rev. J. R. MACDUFF, D.D. Post 8vo, 6s. 6d. cloth.

"Dr. Macduff has rightly appreciated the characters he has described, and has truthfully delineated their features. The points of instruction, too, which he draws from them are apposite, scriptural, and telling."—*Church of England Magazine.*

THE LIGHTHOUSE; or, The Story of a Great Fight between Man and the Sea. By R. M. BALLANTYNE, Author of "The Lifeboat," etc., etc. Illustrations. Crown 8vo, 5s. cloth.

"Interesting to all readers."—*Arbroath Guide.*
"A story at once instructive and amusing."—*Dundee Advertiser.*

FIFTY-TWO SHORT SERMONS FOR FAMILY READING. By HORATIUS BONAR, D.D. Crown 8vo, 6s. cloth.

"These are short plain sermons for family reading, and are admirably fitted for so good a purpose."—*English Presbyterian Messenger.*

THE LIFEBOAT: A Tale of our Coast Heroes. A Book for Boys. By R. M. BALLANTYNE, Author of "The Lighthouse," etc. With Illustrations. Crown 8vo, 5s. cloth.

"This is another of Mr. Ballantyne's excellent stories for the young. They are all well written, full of romantic incidents, and are of no doubtful moral tendency: on the contrary, they are invariably found to embody sentiments of true piety, and manliness and virtue."—*Inverness Advertiser.*

FORGIVENESS, LIFE, AND GLORY. Addresses by S. A. BLACKWOOD, Esq. Small Crown 8vo, 2s. cloth limp; 2s. 6d. cloth boards.

"Full of devout earnestness and scriptural truth."—*Church of England Magazine.*
"They are all solemn and searching.—*Morning Advertiser.*

HYMNS OF FAITH AND HOPE. By HORATIUS BONAR,

D.D. First, Second, and Third Series, Crown 8vo, each 5s. cloth. Also, Pocket Editions, Royal 32mo, each 1s. 6d. Also a Royal Edition, printed at the Chiswick Press, and handsomely bound. Post 8vo, 7s. 6d. cloth.

"There is a freshness and vigour, an earnestness and a piety in these compositions, which is very gratifying. The language is highly poetical."—*Evangelical Christendom.*

THE POEMS OF GEORGE HERBERT. Illustrated

in the highest style of Wood Engraving, by Birket Foster, Clayton, and Noel Humphreys. Post 4to, 12s. cloth elegant.

"There have been many editions of Herbert's Poetical Works. One of the most splendid is that of Nisbet, London."—*Encyclopædia Britannica.*

ILLUSTRATIVE GATHERINGS FOR PREACH-

ERS AND TEACHERS. By the Rev. G. S. BOWES, B.A. First and Second Series, Small Crown 8vo, each, 3s. 6d. cloth.

"Its tone is thoroughly evangelical and spiritual, and it is fitted to furnish useful hints and illustrations to the Christian teacher."—*Christian Witness.*

ENGLISH HEARTS AND ENGLISH HANDS; or,

The Railway and the Trenches. By the Author of "Memorials of Captain Hedley Vicars." Small Crown 8vo, 5s. cloth. Also a Cheaper Edition, 2s. cloth limp.

"The Memorials of Vicars and these Memorials of the Crystal Palace Navvies are books of precisely the same type, and must not be overlooked. We recognize in them an honesty of purpose, a purity of heart, and a warmth of human affection, combined with a religious faith, that are very beautiful."—*Times.*

THE EXETER HALL LECTURES TO YOUNG

MEN, from their commencement in 1845-6, to their termination in 1864-5, all uniformly printed, and handsomely bound in cloth, and embellished with portraits of the Friends and Patrons of the Young Men's Christian Association. Complete in 20 vols., price of each volume, 4s.; or the whole series for £3.

MATTHEW HENRY'S COMMENTARY ON THE

HOLY BIBLE, comprising upwards of 7000 Pages, well printed (the Notes as well as the Text in clear and distinct type) on good paper, forming Nine Imperial 8vo volumes, and handsomely bound in cloth. Price £3 3s. cloth.

*** The work may also be had in a variety of extra bindings, of which a list will be forwarded on application.

THE REV. THOS. SCOTT'S COMMENTARY ON

THE HOLY BIBLE, comprising Marginal References, a copious Topical Index, Fifteen Maps, and Sixty-nine Engravings, illustrative of Scripture Incidents and Scenery. Complete in 6 vols. 4to, published at £4 4s., now offered for £2 10s.

THE BIBLE MANUAL: an Expository and Practical

Commentary on the Books of Scripture, arranged in Chronological Order: forming a Hand-book of Biblical Elucidation for the use of Families, Schools, and Students of the Word of God. Translated from the German Work, edited by the late Rev. Dr. C. G. BARTH, of Calw, Wurtemberg. Imperial 8vo, 12s. cloth.

THE WORD SERIES.

By ELIZABETH WETHERALL and ANNA LOTHROP, Authors of "The Wide Wide World," "Dollars and Cents," etc. Uniform with the "Golden Ladder" Series, with Coloured Illustrations. Crown 8vo, each 3s. 6d. cloth.

"The aim of this series of volumes is so to set forth the Bible incidents and course of history, with its train of actors, as to see them in the circumstances and colouring, the light and shade of their actual existence."

1. WALKS FROM EDEN: The Scripture Story from the Creation to the Death of Abraham.
2. THE HOUSE OF ISRAEL: The Scripture Story from the Birth of Isaac to the Death of Jacob.
3. THE STAR OUT OF JACOB: The Scripture Story Illustrating the Earlier Portion of the Gospel Narrative.

THE GOLDEN LADDER SERIES.

Uniform in size and binding, with eight coloured Illustrations. Crown 8vo, cloth.

1. THE GOLDEN LADDER: Stories Illustrative of the Eight Beatitudes. By ELIZABETH and ANNA WARNER. 3s. 6d.
2. THE WIDE WIDE WORLD. By ELIZABETH WARNER. 3s. 6d.
3. QUEECHY. By the same. 3s. 6d.
4. MELBOURNE HOUSE. By the same. 3s. 6d.
5. DAISY. By the same. 3s. 6d.
6. THE OLD HELMET. By the same. 3s. 6d.
7. THE THREE LITTLE SPADES. By the same. 2s. 6d.
8. NETTIE'S MISSION: Stories Illustrative of the Lord's Prayer. By ALICE GRAY 3s. 6d.
9. DAISY IN THE FIELD. By ELIZABETH WARNER. 3s. 6d.
10. STEPPING HEAVENWARD. By Mrs. PRENTISS. Author of "Little Susy." 2s. 6d.
11. WHAT SHE COULD, AND OPPORTUNITIES. Tales by ELIZABETH WARNER. 3s. 6d.
12. GLEN LUNA; or, Dollars and Cents. By ANNA WARNER. 3s. 6d.
13. DRAYTON HALL. Stories Illustrative of the Beatitudes. ALICE GRAY. 3s. 6d.
14. WITHOUT AND WITHIN. A New England Story. 3s. 6d.
15. VINEGAR HILL STORIES. Illustrative of the Parable of the Sower. By ANNA WARNER. 3s. 6d.
16. THE HOUSE IN TOWN. A Sequel to "Opportunities." By ELIZABETH WARNER. 2s. 6d.
17. LITTLE SUNBEAMS. Stories by JOANNA H. MATTHEWS. 3s. 6d.

THE ONE SHILLING JUVENILE SERIES.

Uniform in size and binding, 16mo, Illustrations, each 1s. cloth.

1. CHANGES UPON CHURCH BELLS. By C. S. H.
2. GONZALEZ AND HIS WAKING DREAMS. By C. S. H.
3. DAISY BRIGHT. By Emma Marshall.
4. HELEN; or, Temper and its Consequences. By Mrs. G. Gladstone.
5. THE CAPTAIN'S STORY; or, The Disobedient Son. By W. S. Martin.
6. THE LITTLE PEATCUTTERS; or, The Song of Love. By Emma Marshall.
7. LITTLE CROWNS, AND HOW TO WIN THEM. By the Rev. J. A. Collier.
8. CHINA AND ITS PEOPLE. By a Missionary's Wife.
9. TEDDY'S DREAM; or, A Little Sweep's Mission.
10. ELDER PARK; or, Scenes in our Garden. By Mrs. Alfred Payne, Author of "Nature's Wonders."
11. HOME LIFE AT GREYSTONE LODGE. By the Author of "Agnes Falconer."
12. THE PEMBERTON FAMILY, and other Stories.
13. CHRISTMAS AT SUNBURY DALE. By W. B. B., Author of "Clara Downing's Dream."
14. PRIMROSE; or, The Bells of Old Effingham. By Mrs. Marshall.
15. THE BOY GUARDIAN. By the Author of "Dick and his Donkey."
16. VIOLET'S IDOL. By Joanna H. Matthews.
17. FRANK GORDON. By the Author of "The Young Marooners." And LITTLE JACK'S FOUR LESSONS. By the Author of "The Golden Ladder."
18. THE COTTAGE ON THE CREEK. By the Hon. Mrs. Clifford-Butler.
19. THE WILD BELLS AND WHAT THEY RANG. By W. S. Martin.
20. TO-DAY AND YESTERDAY. A Story of Winter and Summer Holidays. By Mrs. Marshall.
21. GLASTONBURY; or the early British Christians. By Mrs. Alfred Payne.
22. MAX; a Story of the Oberstein Forest.

THE EIGHTEENPENNY JUVENILE SERIES.

Uniform in size and binding, 16mo, with Illustrations, each 1s. 6d. cloth.

---

1. AUNT EDITH; or, Love to God the Best Motive.
2. SUSY'S SACRIFICE. By Alice Gray.
3. KENNETH FORBES; or, Fourteen Ways of Studying the Bible.
4. LILIES OF THE VALLEY, and other Tales.
5. CLARA STANLEY; or, a Summer among the Hills.
6. THE CHILDREN OF BLACKBERRY HOLLOW.
7. HERBERT PERCY; or, From Christmas to Easter.
8. PASSING CLOUDS; or, Love conquering Evil.
9. DAYBREAK; or, Right Struggling and Triumphant.
10. WARFARE AND WORK; or, Life's Progress.
11. EVELYN GREY. By the Author of "Clara Stanley."
12. THE HISTORY OF THE GRAVELYN FAMILY.
13. DONALD FRASER. By the Author of "Bertie Lee."
14. THE SAFE COMPASS, AND HOW IT POINTS. By Rev. R. Newton, D.D.
15. THE KING'S HIGHWAY; or, Illustrations of the Commandments. By the same.
16. BESSIE AT THE SEASIDE. By Joanna H. Matthews.
17. CASPER. By the Authors of "The Wide Wide World," etc.
18. KARL KRINKEN; or, The Christmas Stocking. By the same.
19. MR. RUTHERFORD'S CHILDREN. By the same.
20. SYBIL AND CHRYSSA. By the same.

THE EIGHTEENPENNY JUVENILE SERIES—*Continued*.

21. HARD MAPLE. By the same.
22. OUR SCHOOL DAYS. Edited by C. S. H.
23. AUNT MILDRED'S LEGACY. By the Author of "The Best Cheer," etc.
24. MAGGIE AND BESSIE, AND THEIR WAY TO DO GOOD. By Joanna H. Matthews.
25. GRACE BUXTON; or, The Light of Home. By Emma Marshall.
26. LITTLE KATY AND JOLLY JIM. By Alice Gray.
27. BESSIE AT SCHOOL. By Joanna H. Matthews.
28. BESSIE AND HER FRIENDS. By the same.
29. BESSIE IN THE MOUNTAINS. By the same.
30. HILDA AND HILDEBRAND; or, The Twins of Ferndale Abbey.
31. GLEN ISLA. By Mrs. Drummond.
32. LUCY SEYMOUR; or, "It is more Blessed to give than to receive." By the same.
33. LOUISA MORETON; or, "Children, obey your Parents in all things." By the same.
34. THE WILMOT FAMILY; or, "They that deal truly are His delight." By the same.
35. SOWING IN TEARS, AND REAPING IN JOY. By Franz Hoffmann. Translated from the German by Mrs. Faber.
36. BESSIE ON HER TRAVELS. By Joanna H. Matthews.
37. LITTLE NELLIE; or, The Clockmaker's Daughter.
38. THREE LITTLE SISTERS. By Mrs. Marshall, Author of "Daisy Bright."
39. MABEL GRANT. A Highland Story.
40. THE RETURN FROM INDIA. By the Author of "Hilda and Hildebrand," &c.
41. THE COURT AND THE KILN. A Story founded on the Church Catechism.
42. SILVER SANDS. By G. E. E. Crampton.
43. LIONEL ST CLAIR. By the Author of "Herbert Percy."

THE SELECT SERIES.

Crown 8vo, each 3s. 6d. cloth. Bound by BURN. Most of them with Illustrations.

1. DERRY. A Tale of the Revolution. By CHARLOTTE ELIZABETH.
2. THE LAND OF THE FORUM AND THE VATICAN. By the Rev. NEWMAN HALL, LL.B.
3. THE LISTENER. By CAROLINE FRY.
4. DAYS AND NIGHTS IN THE EAST; or, Illustrations of Bible Scenes. By the Rev. HORATIUS BONAR, D.D.
5. BEECHENHURST. A Tale. By A. G., Author of "Among the Mountains," etc.
6. THE HOLY WAR. By JOHN BUNYAN.
7. THE PILGRIM'S PROGRESS. By JOHN BUNYAN.
8. THE MOUNTAINS OF THE BIBLE; Their Scenes and their Lessons. By the Rev. JOHN MACFARLANE, LL.D.
9. THROUGH DEEP WATERS; or, Seeking and Finding. An Autobiography.
10. HOME AND FOREIGN SERVICE; or, Pictures in Active Christian Life.
11. LIFE. A Series of Illustrations of the Divine Wisdom in the Forms, Structures, and Instincts of Animals. By PHILLIP H. GOSSE, F.R.S.
12. LAND AND SEA. By P. H. GOSSE, F.R.S.
13. JOHN KNOX AND HIS TIMES. By the Author of "The Story of Martin Luther," etc.
14. HOME IN THE HOLY LAND. By Mrs. FINN.
15. A THIRD YEAR IN JERUSALEM. A Tale Illustrating Incidents and Customs in Modern Jerusalem. By Mrs. FINN.
16 & 17. THE ROMANCE OF NATURAL HISTORY. By P. H. GOSSE, F.R.S. First and Second Series.
18. BYEWAYS IN PALESTINE. By JAMES FINN, Esq. F.R.A.S., late H. M. Consul of Jerusalem and Palestine.
19. HEADS AND TALES; or, Anecdotes and Stories of Quadrupeds and other Beasts, as connected with the Histories of more or less distinguished men. Selected and written by ADAM WHITE, Duddingston.
20. BLOOMFIELD. A Tale by ELIZABETH WARREN, Author of "John Knox and his Times," &c.
21. TALES FROM ALSACE; or, Scenes and Portraits from Life in the Days of the Reformation, as drawn from old Chronicles. Translated from the German.
22. HYMNS OF THE CHURCH MILITANT. By the Author of "The Wide Wide World."
23. THE PHYSICIAN'S DAUGHTERS; or, The Spring Time of Woman. By the Author of "Wandering Homes and their Influences," &c.

Henderson, Rait, & Fenton, Printers, 23, Berners Street, Oxford Street.

www.ingramcontent.com/pod-product-compliance
Lightning Source LLC
Chambersburg PA
CBHW020224240426
43672CB00006B/404